THE NORTHWEST BEST PLACES
COOKBOOK

THE NORTHWEST BEST PLACES

COOKBOOK

Recipes

from the Outstanding

Restaurants and Inns of

Washington, Oregon, and

British Columbia

Cynthia C. Nims & Lori McKean

SASQUATCH BOOKS

SEATTLE

Printed in the United States of America.
Distributed in Canada by Raincoast Books Ltd.
06 05 04 03 02 01   11 10 9 8 7

Cover and interior design: Karen Schober
Cover photo: Rosanne Olson
Interior illustrations: Pauline Cilmi Speers
Composition: Kate Basart
Copy editing: Rebecca Pepper and Alice Copp Smith
Index: Sigrid Asmus

Library of Congress Cataloging in Publication Data
Nims, Cynthia.
The Northwest best places cookbook : recipes from the outstanding restaurants and inns of
Washington, Oregon, and British Columbia / Cynthia Nims, Lori McKean.
        p.   cm.
        Includes index.
        ISBN 1-57061-075-4 (pbk.)
        1. Cookery, American—Pacific Northwest style. I. McKean, Lori.
II. Title.
TX715.2.P32N56   1996
641.59795—dc20   96-13187

Sasquatch Books
615 Second Avenue
Seattle, Washington 98104
(206)467-4300
books@SasquatchBooks.com
www.SasquatchBooks.com

CONTENTS

ACKNOWLEDGMENTS

Many thanks to our local chefs, winemakers, growers,

and producers for making the Northwest one of the most delicious regions in the world.

The authors also gratefully acknowledge the recipe-testing help they received from Susan Fowler

Volland, Gwendolyn Hayes, and Tim and Katherine Kehrli. Thanks from Cynthia to Bob

for his never-ending willingness to be on the tasting end of the tests;

thanks from Lori to Tony for his vision and inspiration.

INTRODUCTION

For over twenty years, *Northwest Best Places®* has been guiding discriminating diners and travelers to the best food and accommodations in Oregon, Washington, and British Columbia. Now the fine foods of the Northwest have come home to you. Sasquatch Books, publisher of the *Best Places* travel guides, asked us to create a cookbook based on the recipes of the establishments (restaurants, bakeries, inns, hotels, and bed and breakfasts) included in *Northwest Best Places*. The intent was to assemble a cookbook that would reflect the diversity of the region—one that would showcase the culinary savvy involved in a dish like Dungeness Crab Wontons from Lincoln City's Bay House, and the down-home basics of a staple like Cranberry Pot Roast from the Tokeland Hotel.

We invited every establishment featured in the 21st edition of *Northwest Best Places* to submit a favorite recipe or two. From there, we sifted through the hundreds of responses to find the 125 recipes that would both represent the region's best and offer a balanced range of dishes, meals, and tastes. In the process, we gleaned treasures of regional cooking traditions and lore from the Northwest's most adventurous kitchens.

Stories about Northwest culinary heritage invariably reveal links between the land and its seasons. One contributor wrote enthusiastically about the first morels of spring; another about harvest time in autumn. Others applauded Northwesterners' willingness to experiment with ingredients. Typical of the curiosity and daring found in so many of these recipes are Columbia Gorge Hotel Chef Fritton Unkefer's Seared Sea Scallops with Huckleberry Lavender Vinaigrette and Wild Chanterelle Mushrooms, and Friday Harbor House Chef Greg Atkinson's fragrant Nootka Rose Petal Ice Cream.

In *The Northwest Best Places Cookbook*, the ingredients are the true stars. Regardless of the diversity of their dishes, all chefs agreed on one thing: superior ingredients are essential to the success of their recipes. And for bounty, quality, and flavor, there's no need to leave the region. The Pacific Northwest's own particular blend of sun, rain, rich farmlands, outstanding vineyards, and clean, nutrient-rich waters produces a dynamic array of ingredients for the creative chef. The region is renowned for its salmon, oysters, wild mushrooms, apples, asparagus, onions, and cranberries, among others.

All of the elements of Northwest cuisine are present here—excellent ingredients in the hands of the most creative chefs—and now you can prepare the best of the region in your own home.

BREAKFAST

MOUNT ADAMS
HUCKLEBERRY HOTCAKES

The Flying L Ranch, Glenwood, Washington

Forty years ago, Ilse Lloyd presided over the stove at the Flying L Ranch. Today her sons Darvel and Darryl Lloyd still flip out the hotcakes bubbling with berries picked from the nearby huckleberry fields. "Business was a lot slower in the old days," recall Darvel and Darryl. "Back then, Mother had time to pick the berries in the foothills of Mount Adams, fix breakfast, clean the rooms, saddle up the horses, take our guests for an evening ride, and maybe even cook 'em dinner!"

3 cups all-purpose flour	*4 eggs*
¾ cup rolled oats	*4 cups buttermilk, more if needed*
¼ cup oat bran or 100% bran cereal	*¼ cup vegetable oil*
4 teaspoons baking powder	*1 to 2 cups huckleberries, fresh or frozen*
2 teaspoons baking soda	*(blueberries make a good substitute)*
½ teaspoon salt (optional)	

STIR TOGETHER THE FLOUR, oats, oat bran or bran cereal, baking powder, baking soda, and salt in a large bowl. In another bowl, beat the eggs, then stir in the buttermilk and oil. Add the egg mixture to the flour mixture and stir gently until just blended. If the batter is too thick, stir in a little more buttermilk.

HEAT A GRIDDLE or a large, heavy skillet, preferably nonstick (brush lightly with oil if it is not nonstick). Stir the huckleberries into the batter. Pour ¼ cup batter onto the griddle for each pancake. Cook until bubbly on top, then flip and continue cooking until nicely browned. Serve with your favorite syrup or fresh fruit jam.

Makes 6 to 8 servings

SMOKED SALMON
and Chive Potato Pancakes

Inn at Swifts Bay, Lopez Island, Washington

"Firm, hot-smoked salmon works best in this recipe," says innkeeper
Christopher Brandmeir, who serves a poached egg, cooked with Old Bay
seasoning and vinegar, along with these hearty pancakes. Note that the cottage
cheese and ricotta topping must be prepared the night before.

PANCAKES

3 pounds large white or russet potatoes	*1 teaspoon Old Bay seasoning*
3 eggs, lightly beaten	*½ teaspoon baking powder*
½ cup chopped chives, plus more for garnish	*¼ teaspoon freshly ground black pepper*
½ cup finely chopped onion	*6 to 8 ounces hot-smoked salmon, skin and*
⅓ cup all-purpose flour or potato flour	*bones removed, finely chopped*
2 teaspoons no-salt seafood seasoning mix,	*1 to 2 tablespoons olive oil*
such as Marketspice brand	*Grated lemon zest, for garnish*

TOPPING

1 cup nonfat cottage cheese	*1 teaspoon freshly squeezed lemon juice,*
¼ cup nonfat, low-salt ricotta cheese	*or to taste*

PREPARE THE TOPPING the night before serving. Combine the cottage cheese
and ricotta in a colander and let sit for at least 1 hour to drain slightly. Place the cheeses
in a food processor with the lemon juice and process until very smooth, about 3 minutes.
Taste for tartness, adding more lemon juice to taste. Transfer to a bowl and refrigerate
overnight to thicken.

FOR THE PANCAKES, peel the potatoes and grate them. Rinse them in a colander in cold water (or in fruit fresh—a commercial whitener that will prevent them from graying), then wrap them in a dish towel and squeeze to remove all excess moisture. In a large bowl, combine the eggs, chives, onion, flour, seafood seasoning, Old Bay seasoning, baking powder, and pepper. Stir in the salmon and potatoes. Line a baking sheet with cut-up brown paper bags for holding the cooked pancakes.

HEAT A LARGE FRYING PAN, preferably nonstick, with some of the olive oil. Stir the potato mixture again and scoop a few pancakes into the pan, using about ¼ cup batter for each pancake. Flatten them with a spatula. Cook until nicely browned, about 2 to 3 minutes per side. Transfer the potato pancakes to the paper-lined baking sheet and keep warm in a low oven. Continue with the remaining potato mixture.

TO SERVE, arrange 3 potato pancakes on each individual warmed plate. Scoop a generous spoonful of the topping over the pancakes and sprinkle with chopped chives and lemon zest.

Makes 6 servings

WILD BLACKBERRY COFFEE CAKE

Eagles Nest Inn, Langley, Washington

Packed with plump, juicy blackberries, this coffee cake is a favorite during
the summer months at the Eagles Nest Inn, where blackberries abound. Frozen
blackberries can be substituted for fresh; however, if you use frozen berries, plan to
bake the cake for an extra 20 minutes. What you don't finish in the morning will
keep well for an afternoon snack or evening dessert, even a day or two later.

COFFEE CAKE

⅓ cup packed brown sugar	*¼ cup butter, melted and cooled slightly*
⅓ cup chopped walnuts	*1 egg*
2½ cups sifted all-purpose flour	*½ teaspoon almond extract or vanilla extract*
½ cup granulated sugar	*¼ teaspoon ground nutmeg*
2 teaspoons baking powder	*⅓ cup shredded coconut*
¼ teaspoon salt	*2 cups fresh wild blackberries or frozen whole*
1 cup milk	*blackberries (do not thaw if frozen)*

GLAZE

½ cup powdered sugar | *2 teaspoons milk*

PREHEAT THE OVEN to 375°F. Lightly grease the bottom and sides of a 9-inch
round, deep baking dish such as a quiche dish.

STIR TOGETHER the brown sugar and walnuts in a small bowl; set aside.

COMBINE THE FLOUR, granulated sugar, baking powder, and salt in a large bowl. Whisk in the milk, melted butter, egg, almond or vanilla extract, and nutmeg until smooth and well mixed. Spread about two-thirds of the batter in the prepared pan. Sprinkle the coconut evenly over it. Scatter half of the blackberries over the batter, pushing them slightly into it.

SPOON THE REMAINING BATTER into the dish, gently spreading it toward the edges; you don't need to cover the berries completely. Scatter the remaining berries over the top. Sprinkle the brown sugar and walnuts evenly over the berries. Bake until a toothpick inserted in the center comes out clean, 40 to 45 minutes. Let cool.

FOR THE GLAZE, combine the powdered sugar and milk in a small bowl and stir until the sugar dissolves. Drizzle the glaze over the coffee cake, beginning in the center and working in a spiral toward the outer edge. Cut into wedges and serve.

Makes 8 servings

APPLE-ONION OMELET

State Street Inn Bed & Breakfast, Hood River, Oregon

Packed with sweet onions and apples, this omelet offers
a refreshing change for breakfast. It's best when served with buttered
toast and hash browns or fried red potatoes.

3 eggs	*¾ cup very thinly sliced onion,*
¼ cup milk	*preferably Walla Walla Sweet*
1 tablespoon water	*1 large semisweet apple, such as Jonagold,*
Salt and freshly ground black pepper	*Gala, or McIntosh, peeled, cored, and*
1 tablespoon butter	*thinly sliced*
	½ cup grated cheddar cheese

PREHEAT THE OVEN to 400°F.

BEAT THE EGGS with the milk and water in a small bowl. Add a pinch each of salt
and pepper.

MELT THE BUTTER in a small ovenproof omelet pan or skillet over medium heat.
Add the onion and apple and sauté until the onion begins to turn translucent, about 5
to 6 minutes. Spread the onion–apple mixture evenly in the pan and sprinkle the cheese
over it. Pour the egg mixture evenly into the pan and cook over medium heat until the
edges are beginning to set. Transfer the pan to the oven and bake until the center is
firmly set, 10 to 12 minutes.

CUT THE OMELET in half and slide each half onto an individual plate.
Serve immediately.

Makes 2 servings

GROVELAND COTTAGE HOT CEREAL

Groveland Cottage, Dungeness, Washington

This hearty breakfast cereal is delicious accented with brown
sugar and a touch of cream or plain yogurt. You can vary it by using
apple juice in place of the water for cooking the grains and topping the cereal
with chopped fresh or sautéed apples. For the mixed grains, Simone Nichols
of the Groveland suggests equal parts rolled thick oats, triticale, rye,
and red wheat with one-half part barley.

4 cups water	*¼ cup currants or dark raisins*
2 cups mixed grains	*1 tablespoon ground cinnamon*
(see recipe introduction, above)	*½ teaspoon salt*
¼ cup golden raisins	*½ cup chopped walnuts*

BRING THE WATER to a boil in a large saucepan. Stir in the grains, raisins, currants,
cinnamon, and salt. Scatter the walnuts on top, but do not stir them in. Reduce the heat
to low, cover the pan, and cook gently until the grains are tender, about 45 minutes. Stir
and serve.

Makes 4 to 6 servings

BLUEBERRY SCONES

River Run Cottages, Ladner, British Columbia

Guests at the floating River Run Cottages, located on the Fraser
River in historic Ladner, often borrow bikes and go blueberry picking
on nearby Westam Island. The innkeepers welcome any leftover berries,
which they turn into their favorite blueberry scones. If blueberries aren't
available, huckleberries, currants, or raisins make good substitutions.

¾ cup half-and-half	*¼ cup sugar*
⅓ cup blueberries (fresh or frozen)	*1 tablespoon baking powder*
1 egg, lightly beaten	*½ teaspoon salt*
2¼ cups all-purpose flour	*½ cup unsalted butter, cut in pieces*

PREHEAT THE OVEN to 350°F. Lightly grease a baking sheet.

STIR TOGETHER the half-and-half, blueberries, and egg in a small bowl. Sift the flour,
sugar, baking powder, and salt into a large bowl. Cut in the butter, using a pastry cutter
or two table knives, until the mixture resembles fine crumbs. Alternatively, put the dry
ingredients in a food processor, add the butter, and pulse a few times to cut the butter
into the flour; then transfer the mixture to a bowl.

ADD THE BLUEBERRY mixture to the flour mixture and gently stir until just
blended. Turn the dough onto a lightly floured surface and knead lightly a few times.
Pat the dough into a rectangle about 6 inches by 10 inches. Cut the dough into 10
scones, each 2 inches by 3 inches, and set them on the baking sheet. Bake until puffed
and golden brown, 15 to 20 minutes.

Makes 10 scones

BERRY SENSE

Plump, juicy, and fresh from the bush or vine, berries are some of nature's sweetest, healthiest, and most delicious foods. Berries are low in calories, averaging about 80 per cup, and are packed with vitamins, potassium, iron, and calcium. Fresh berries are also an excellent source of natural fiber.

When selecting berries, choose firm, plump fruit that is brightly colored and full flavored. Berries will keep for several days in the refrigerator but are best when freshly picked. Don't wash berries until it's time to use them. Wash gently and thoroughly under cold water and drain on paper towels. To prevent strawberries from absorbing water, don't hull them until they have been washed and dried. Raspberries and other hollow berries often benefit from being dropped gently on a towel to release any bugs that may be hiding inside.

Caneberries, including blackberries, raspberries, salmonberries, and so on, freeze well: Simply wash the berries, then lay them in a single layer on a tray or cookie sheet. Freeze until firm, then pack the berries into freezer bags or containers and return to the freezer. They will keep for up to nine months.

GINGERBREAD CREPES
with Apple Filling

Quimper Inn, Port Townsend, Washington

This fall recipe is good any time of year. You'll need only eight crepes
for this recipe, so don't worry if the first few don't work out. Extra crepes can
be wrapped in plastic wrap and foil and frozen for later use. Tart, firm
apples, such as Gravensteins or Granny Smiths, work best.

CREPES

1 cup all-purpose flour	1⅓ cups milk
1 to 2 tablespoons sugar	2 eggs
1 teaspoon powdered ginger	¼ cup molasses
1 teaspoon ground cinnamon	1 tablespoon butter, melted, plus
Pinch ground cloves	more for cooking the crepes

APPLE FILLING

¼ cup butter	1 tablespoon ground cinnamon, or more to taste
3 large, firm apples, peeled, cored, and sliced	Unsweetened whipped cream, for serving
½ cup hot water	Chopped walnuts, for serving
¼ cup sugar	

FOR THE CREPES, combine the flour, sugar, ginger, cinnamon, and cloves in a large
bowl. In another bowl, combine the milk, eggs, molasses, and melted butter. Make a
shallow well in the center of the dry mixture, add the wet mixture, and stir gently just
until well combined.

HEAT ABOUT 2 TEASPOONS butter in a crepe pan or small skillet, preferably non-stick, over medium heat. Add about ¼ cup of the crepe batter, tilting the pan so it evenly covers the bottom. Cook until the top is set and the edges begin to brown, 1 to 2 minutes. Turn the crepe and continue cooking just until the other side is lightly browned, about 1 minute longer. Turn the crepe onto a plate and continue with the remaining batter, adding more butter as necessary. Put a piece of waxed paper or plastic wrap over each crepe to make them easier to separate later. The crepes can be made a day in advance and refrigerated, covered.

FOR THE APPLE FILLING, melt the butter in a large skillet, add the apple slices, and cook, stirring, until they are well coated in butter, 1 to 2 minutes. Add the water, sugar, and cinnamon and continue cooking, uncovered, until the apples are tender but not mushy, 12 to 15 minutes longer. The sauce should be syrupy; add a little more water if needed.

TO ASSEMBLE THE CREPES, reheat them, if necessary, in a low oven. Lay some of the apple slices down the center of each crepe and roll it up. Arrange 2 filled crepes on each plate and drizzle with a little of the sauce from the apples. Top the crepes with a dollop of whipped cream and a sprinkle of chopped walnuts. Serve immediately.

Makes 4 servings

CINNAMON BUNS

The Old Farmhouse, Salt Spring Island, British Columbia

These giant cinnamon rolls, enhanced with fruits and spices, will arouse your morning tastebuds. Innkeeper Gertie Fuss invented these power breakfast rolls, which receive raves from her guests at this three-star island inn.

1 small navel orange	⅓ cup buttermilk
⅓ cup warm water	¼ cup sour cream
2 tablespoons (2 packages) active dry yeast	6 cups all-purpose flour, more if needed
½ cup plus 1 tablespoon granulated sugar	2 eggs
¾ cup milk	1 teaspoon salt
½ cup butter	

FILLING

½ cup butter, softened	2 tablespoons ground cinnamon
¾ cup packed brown sugar	2 small apples, peeled, cored, and thinly sliced
¾ cup raisins	

GLAZE

½ cup powdered sugar | 2 tablespoons freshly squeezed orange juice

WASH THE RIND of the orange and cut the orange in quarters. Purée the entire orange in a food processor until smooth. Set aside.

STIR TOGETHER the warm water, yeast, and 1 tablespoon of the sugar in a small bowl. Let sit until frothy, 8 to 10 minutes.

COMBINE THE MILK, butter, buttermilk, and sour cream in a medium saucepan and warm over low heat until the butter is melted. Set aside to cool until the mixture is lukewarm.

COMBINE 1 CUP of the flour with the remaining ½ cup sugar, eggs, orange pulp, salt, and warm milk mixture in the large bowl of an electric mixer. Beat thoroughly. Add the yeast mixture and beat for 2 to 3 minutes longer. Add another cup of flour and continue beating for another minute.

BEGIN ADDING the remaining flour, ½ cup at a time, beating until the dough is smooth and supple. (When the dough begins to form a ball, change to the dough hook attachment if your machine has one.) Avoid adding too much flour; it's better the dough be a little sticky than too dry. Cover the bowl with a damp cloth and let rise in a warm place until doubled in bulk, about 1 hour.

PUNCH DOWN THE DOUGH, set it on a lightly floured work surface, and roll it into a rectangle about ½ inch thick (roughly 16 inches by 20 inches). Spread the softened butter over the dough and sprinkle evenly with the brown sugar, raisins, and cinnamon. Arrange the apple slices in lengthwise rows over the filling. Roll the dough up into a cylinder and slice it into 12 pieces, each about 1½ inches thick. Arrange the slices on two lightly greased baking sheets, with at least 1 inch between the buns. Cover with a cloth and let rise for 45 minutes to 1 hour.

PREHEAT THE OVEN to 350°F.

BAKE THE CINNAMON BUNS until nicely browned and puffed, about 8 to 12 minutes. Meanwhile, stir together the powdered sugar and orange juice for the glaze. When the cinnamon buns come from the oven, drizzle the glaze over them and let cool slightly. Serve warm.

Makes 12 buns

DUNGENESS CRAB QUICHE

Groveland Cottage, Dungeness, Washington

Sweet, meaty Dungeness crab is the house specialty at this bed
and breakfast located on Dungeness Way, in Dungeness, Washington, a small
fishing village on the Strait of Juan de Fuca. Besides crab, this recipe calls for
chanterelle mushrooms, but you can substitute common button
mushrooms if wild mushrooms are not available.

½ pound chanterelles, cleaned,
trimmed, and coarsely chopped
4 shallots, minced
1 tablespoon butter
1 tablespoon olive oil
2 tablespoons dried dill weed
1 tablespoon freshly squeezed lemon juice
Salt and hot pepper sauce or freshly
ground black pepper

2 cups Dungeness crabmeat
(about ¾ pound)
3 eggs
1 cup half-and-half
½ cup grated Parmesan cheese
2 tablespoons minced cilantro or flat-leaf
(Italian) parsley, for garnish

PASTRY CRUST

1½ cups all-purpose flour
6 tablespoons butter, cut in pieces

½ teaspoon salt
3 tablespoons chilled water (more if needed)

FOR THE CRUST, combine the flour, butter, and salt in a food processor and process
until the mixture has the texture of coarse crumbs. Add the water and pulse until the
mixture just begins to form a ball, adding a little more water if needed. Turn the dough
onto a work surface, form it into a ball, and wrap it in plastic. Chill for at least 1 hour.

PREHEAT THE OVEN to 375°F.

ON A LIGHTLY FLOURED work surface, roll the dough into a circle about 14 inches in diameter. Line a 10-inch pie pan with the dough, fluting the edges and trimming the excess as necessary. Place a sheet of foil over the dough and cover the bottom with pie weights or dried beans. Bake the crust for 10 minutes; remove the foil and weights and continue baking until it is set and lightly browned, 18 to 20 minutes. Let cool.

REDUCE THE OVEN to 350°F.

HEAT A NONSTICK SKILLET over medium-high heat, add the mushrooms, and cook until they become tender and the liquid they release has evaporated, about 5 minutes. Add the shallots, butter, and oil and sauté until the shallots are tender but not browned, 2 to 3 minutes. Stir in the dill and lemon juice, adding salt and hot pepper sauce to taste. Take the skillet from the heat.

PICK OVER THE CRABMEAT to remove any bits of shell or cartilage. Add it to the skillet and stir until well mixed; set aside.

IN A MEDIUM BOWL, combine the eggs with the half-and-half and all but 2 table-spoons of the Parmesan cheese.

SPREAD THE CRAB MIXTURE evenly in the pie shell. Pour the egg mixture over it and sprinkle the reserved Parmesan cheese over the top. Bake until a knife inserted into the quiche comes out clean, 35 to 40 minutes. Remove from the oven, sprinkle with the cilantro, and let sit 5 minutes before cutting to serve.

Makes 8 servings

MARY'S OATMEAL PANCAKES

Salisbury House, Seattle, Washington

For these surprisingly light and fluffy pancakes, the oats
soak in buttermilk overnight; they offer body, texture, and a certain richness
to the batter without weighing it down. Top the pancakes off with real
maple syrup and sour cream or yogurt.

2 cups rolled oats	*1 teaspoon baking powder*
3 cups buttermilk	*¼ teaspoon salt*
½ cup all-purpose flour	*2 eggs, lightly beaten*
1 teaspoon baking soda	*¼ cup vegetable oil*

CHUNKY APPLESAUCE

3 Golden Delicious apples,	*¼ cup granulated sugar, or more to taste*
peeled, cored, and sliced	*½ teaspoon ground cinnamon, or more to taste*
⅓ cup water	

THE NIGHT BEFORE making the pancakes, combine the oats and buttermilk in a
large bowl, stir to mix, cover, and refrigerate overnight.

FOR THE APPLESAUCE, combine the apples with the water in a medium saucepan
and cook over low heat until the apples are soft but still holding together, 12 to 15 minutes. Stir in sugar and cinnamon to taste; set aside.

JUST BEFORE SERVING, combine the flour, baking soda, baking powder, and salt in a
large bowl. In another bowl, stir together the eggs and vegetable oil. Add the egg mixture
to the flour mixture, followed by the oatmeal mixture. Stir gently to mix well. Cook the
pancakes on a lightly oiled hot griddle until golden brown, about 2 minutes per side.
Serve hot, with the applesauce on the side.

Makes 4 to 6 servings

WINTER FRUIT COMPOTE

Abigail's Hotel, Victoria, British Columbia

Sprinkled with toasted walnuts, this elegant fruit compote is
great for breakfast or dessert. The recipe calls for Sauternes, a dessert wine
produced in France; however, any of the numerous fine dessert wines from the
Northwest will work equally well. Look for "late harvest" wines that
have been affected by *Botrytis cinerea*, "the noble rot."

¾ cup sugar

½ cup water

½ cup Sauternes or other dessert wine

4 sticks cinnamon

¼ cup freshly squeezed lemon juice

4 Granny Smith apples, peeled, cored,
and cut in 1-inch chunks

1 cup cranberries (fresh or frozen)

4 pears, preferably Bosc, peeled, cored, and cut
in 1-inch chunks

½ cup walnuts, toasted and chopped
in large pieces

COMBINE THE SUGAR, water, Sauternes, cinnamon sticks, and lemon juice in
a large, heavy saucepan. Bring to a boil, stirring often, and boil until reduced by
about one-third, 8 to 10 minutes. Add the apples and cook over medium heat, stirring
occasionally, until just tender, 5 to 6 minutes. Stir in the cranberries and cook for a few
minutes longer. Remove the pan from the heat, stir in the pears, and let sit for a few
minutes until the liquid has cooled slightly. Discard the cinnamon sticks and spoon the
fruit and sauce into individual bowls. Sprinkle the walnuts over the compote and serve.

Makes 4 to 6 servings

FOUR SEASONS BAKED EGGS

Amy's Manor Bed & Breakfast, Pateros, Washington

The 170-acre estate at Amy's Manor includes a farm with
chickens, rabbits, and an organic garden. Breakfasts at the inn always showcase
farm-fresh ingredients, which, like this recipe, change with the seasons.
Be sure to try your own adaptations, using seasonal vegetables and herbs
from your garden or neighborhood market.

BASE RECIPE

8 eggs	Salt and freshly ground black pepper
½ cup half-and-half	1 tablespoon butter, preferably unsalted
⅓ cup sour cream	Herb sprigs, for garnish
¾ cup grated sharp cheddar cheese	

PREHEAT THE OVEN to 350°F.

LIGHTLY WHISK together the eggs, half-and-half, and sour cream. Stir in the cheese
with a pinch each of salt and pepper. Place the butter in a heavy, ovenproof 10-inch
skillet, preferably nonstick, and heat in the oven until melted, about 5 minutes. Take the
pan from the oven and swirl the butter evenly over the bottom of the pan. Add the egg
mixture and bake until the eggs are just set but still moist, 20 to 25 minutes. Let cool for
a few minutes, then slide the eggs onto a cutting board and cut into wedges. Arrange the
wedges on a serving platter or individual plates, garnish with herb sprigs, and serve.

Makes 6 servings

SPRING EGGS

2 cups coarsely chopped arugula, spinach, and/or red mustard leaves | *1 tablespoon minced chives*

AFTER HEATING the pan with the butter, remove it from the oven and add the greens. Toss until wilted, then pour the egg mixture on top, sprinkle the chives over the eggs, and continue as directed in the base recipe.

SUMMER EGGS

Kernels from 1 ear fresh sweet corn | *1 vine-ripe tomato, cut in ¼-inch slices*
8 large basil leaves, finely shredded |

AFTER HEATING the pan with the butter, remove it from the oven and add the corn. Toss until evenly coated in butter. Stir the basil into the egg mixture, then pour it into the pan. Continue as directed in the base recipe, arranging the tomato slices over the eggs after about 15 minutes.

FALL EGGS

1 medium russet potato, scrubbed and cut in ½-inch dice | *2 teaspoons thyme leaves*
| *½ teaspoon dried red pepper flakes*

PLACE THE POTATO in a small pan of lightly salted water, bring to a boil, and cook until nearly tender, 5 to 7 minutes. Drain well.

AFTER HEATING the pan with the butter, remove it from the oven and add the diced potato. Toss until evenly coated in butter. Stir the thyme leaves and red pepper flakes into the egg mixture, then pour it into the pan. Continue as directed in the base recipe.

WINTER EGGS

½ pound bulk pork sausage | *1 teaspoon dried sage leaves, crushed*

COOK THE SAUSAGE in a small skillet over medium heat, breaking it into small pieces, until no pink remains, about 10 minutes. Drain well, discarding the fat.

Stir the sausage and sage into the egg mixture, pour it into the preheated pan, and continue as directed in the base recipe.

PEACH MELBA DUTCH BABY

Commencement Bay Bed & Breakfast, Tacoma, Washington

Hardly any breakfast is as dramatic and delicious as a big, puffy, golden Dutch baby. Innkeeper Sharon Kaufmann varies the fruit topping depending on the season, sometimes combining blackberries with peaches in the summer and using sliced Granny Smith apples sautéed in butter and sugar in the fall and winter.

1 cup raspberries (fresh or frozen)	*1 teaspoon vanilla extract*
3 tablespoons sugar	*½ teaspoon ground cinnamon*
6 tablespoons butter	*½ teaspoon salt*
6 eggs	*2 peaches, peeled, pitted, and sliced*
1½ cups milk	*Fresh raspberries, for garnish*
1 cup all-purpose flour	

PREHEAT THE OVEN to 425°F.

COMBINE THE RASPBERRIES and 1 tablespoon of the sugar in a small saucepan and bring just to a boil over medium heat; alternatively, combine them in a microwave-safe bowl and microwave for about 2 minutes. Gently press the berries through a fine sieve to remove the seeds; set aside to cool.

PLACE THE BUTTER in a 9- by 13-inch baking dish and heat in the oven until the butter melts. Meanwhile, combine the milk, flour, vanilla, cinnamon, and salt with the remaining 2 tablespoons of sugar in a blender and blend until well mixed, about 1 minute. Remove the pan from the oven, slowly pour in the batter, and bake until puffed and golden, 20 to 25 minutes. Remove from the oven and scatter the peach slices over the Dutch baby. Drizzle with the raspberry sauce, garnish with fresh raspberries, and serve warm.

Makes 6 servings

"NUTTY BUT NICE" GRANOLA

Marquee House, Salem, Oregon

Every night at the Marquee House is movie night, featuring
bottomless bowls of popcorn. Inspired by her love for movies and munchies,
owner Rickie Hart created this crunchy breakfast granola, made with popcorn,
hazelnuts, and an assortment of grains. Be sure to use an extra-large
baking pan so that you can stir the granola easily during baking.

¾ cup honey	1 cup chopped hazelnuts
⅓ cup butter	½ cup wheat germ or bran flakes
1 tablespoon water	½ cup crushed shredded wheat cereal
1 teaspoon vanilla extract	½ cup toasted sunflower seeds
3 cups popped popcorn	1 cup golden raisins
4 cups rolled oats	1 cup dried cranberries
1 cup shredded coconut	

PREHEAT THE OVEN to 350°F.

IN A LARGE BAKING PAN (at least 12 by 15 inches and at least 2 inches deep), place
the honey, butter, water, and vanilla. Heat the pan in the oven until the butter is melted,
about 5 minutes.

PUT THE POPPED POPCORN in a food processor and process until finely chopped.
In a large bowl, mix the popcorn, oats, coconut, hazelnuts, wheat germ or bran flakes,
shredded wheat, and sunflower seeds. Remove the pan from the oven and stir the honey
mixture. Add the nuts and grain mixture to the honey and stir to mix well.

BAKE, stirring often, until golden brown, about 40 minutes. Let cool, stirring occasionally
so the granola doesn't clump. Stir in the raisins and cranberries and store in an airtight
container.

Makes 12 generous servings

LEMON CHEESE BRAID

Romeo Inn, Ashland, Oregon

You'll never get the same meal twice at the Romeo Inn, where owners
Bruce and Margaret Halverson keep a computerized list of what they serve
to regular customers. The problem is, once you've tasted their zesty raisin
and cream cheese–filled bread, you might want to eat it again.

1 tablespoon (1 package) active dry yeast	*2 eggs*
¼ cup warm water	*¼ cup granulated sugar*
3 to 4 cups flour	*¼ cup butter, softened*
½ cup milk, scalded and slightly cooled	*½ teaspoon salt*

FILLING

12 ounces cream cheese, softened	*1 teaspoon grated lemon zest*
½ cup granulated sugar	*½ cup raisins*
1 egg	

ICING

½ cup powdered sugar	*1 tablespoon butter, melted*
2 tablespoons freshly squeezed lemon juice	

STIR THE YEAST into the warm water in a small bowl and let sit until frothy, 3 to
4 minutes.

IN THE LARGE BOWL of an electric mixer, combine 2 cups of the flour with the yeast
mixture, milk, eggs, sugar, butter, and salt and mix well. Add enough of the remaining
flour, ¼ cup at a time, to form a soft dough. Knead the dough until very smooth and
elastic, 5 to 10 minutes. Place the dough in a greased bowl, cover, and let rise in a warm
place until doubled in bulk, about 1 hour.

PREPARE THE FILLING while the dough is rising. Using an electric mixer, beat the cream cheese until smooth, gradually adding the sugar. Add the egg and lemon zest and continue beating until well mixed. Stir in the raisins and set aside.

PUNCH DOWN THE DOUGH, place it on a lightly floured work surface, and roll it into a rectangle about 12 inches by 14 inches. Set the dough on a lightly greased baking sheet. Spread the filling lengthwise down the center third of the dough. Using a small, sharp knife or kitchen shears, cut the uncovered outer thirds of the dough in 1-inch strips from the outer edge toward the filling. Beginning at one end, fold the strips over the filling, alternating from side to side, creating a braided effect. Cover and let rise again until doubled in bulk, about 45 minutes.

PREHEAT THE OVEN to 375°F.

BAKE THE BRAID until nicely browned, about 25 minutes. Transfer it to a wire rack to cool.

FOR THE ICING, stir together the powdered sugar, lemon juice, and melted butter until smooth; drizzle over the bread. Cut into slices and serve.

Makes 1 large loaf, 8 to 12 servings

BREAKFAST FRITTATA

Wharfside B&B, Friday Harbor, Washington

Guests who need to catch an early ferry often carry away this
delicious frittata wrapped in a warm tortilla. Hence its nickname, "ferry ta-ta."
This recipe calls for turkey sausage, but any flavorful sausage can be
substituted. For added zest, top the frittata with salsa.

2 tablespoons olive oil	*⅛ teaspoon hot pepper sauce, or to taste*
6 ounces bulk sausage meat, preferably turkey	*Pinch salt*
2 medium red potatoes, cut in ½-inch cubes	*1 tablespoon butter*
6 eggs	*¼ cup diced green onion*
3 tablespoons water	*¼ cup diced red bell pepper*
½ teaspoon minced fresh dill or ¼ teaspoon dried dill weed	*½ cup grated cheddar cheese*
¼ teaspoon lemon pepper or freshly ground black pepper	*¼ cup sour cream*
	Herb sprigs and/or cherry tomatoes, for garnish

HEAT 1 TABLESPOON of the olive oil in a small skillet, add the sausage, and cook
over medium heat, breaking the sausage into small pieces, until no pink remains, about
10 minutes. Drain well, discarding the fat.

BRING A SMALL PAN of water to a boil, add the diced potatoes, and boil for 5 minutes; drain well. In a medium bowl, combine the eggs, water, dill, lemon pepper or black
pepper, hot pepper sauce, and salt.

HEAT THE REMAINING 1 tablespoon olive oil with the butter in a large skillet, preferably nonstick, over medium heat. Add the potatoes and fry until golden and crisp, about 10 minutes. Add the sausage, green onion, and bell pepper and cook for 1 minute longer.

POUR THE EGG MIXTURE over the vegetables and cook over medium heat, gently lifting the edges as the eggs set to help distribute the uncooked egg. Cook, covered, until the eggs are set and the bottom is lightly browned, 3 to 4 minutes.

SLIDE THE FRITTATA onto a serving platter, folding it in half. Sprinkle with grated cheese and add a thick ribbon of sour cream. Garnish with herb sprigs and cherry tomatoes, and serve.

Makes 4 servings

ARTICHOKE SOUFFLÉS

Beaconsfield Inn, Victoria, British Columbia

Soufflés have a reputation for being fussy and difficult to prepare. But
not these. Baked in individual ramekins, they puff to a golden brown when
cooked. Made in larger portions, they would also make a delicious lunch.

6 eggs	*1 can (14 ounces) artichoke hearts,*
¼ teaspoon hot pepper sauce	*drained and coarsely chopped*
¼ cup all-purpose flour	*1 cup grated fontina cheese*
Pinch ground nutmeg	*1 cup grated cheddar cheese*
1½ cups milk	*½ cup chopped green onion or chives*

PREHEAT THE OVEN to 350°F. Lightly grease eight ½-cup ramekins.

WHISK TOGETHER the eggs and hot pepper sauce in a large bowl until blended. Add
the flour and nutmeg and mix well. Whisk in the milk, then stir in the artichoke hearts,
cheeses, and green onion or chives. Spoon the mixture into the ramekins, filling them to
about ¼ inch below the rim. Set the ramekins on a baking sheet and bake until puffed
and nicely browned, 45 to 50 minutes. Serve immediately.

Makes 8 servings

ELVIS PANCAKES

Ram's Head Inn, Rossland, British Columbia

Elvis loved grilled peanut butter and banana sandwiches. But unless
you've stayed at Greg and Tanna Butler's mountain resort in Rossland,
British Columbia, you probably don't know about The King's other favorite—
peanut butter and banana pancakes topped with real maple syrup and butter.
"Elvis requests these pancakes whenever he comes to ski at Red Mountain,"
says Tanna. He may decide to drop in on you, too.

2 eggs	2 tablespoons sugar
2 cups buttermilk	1 teaspoon baking powder
1 cup chunky peanut butter	½ teaspoon salt
¼ cup vegetable oil	2 or 3 ripe bananas, peeled and cut in
1½ cups all-purpose flour (more if necessary)	¼-inch slices

LIGHTLY BEAT the eggs in a large bowl, then add the buttermilk, peanut butter, and
oil and whisk until well mixed. Sift together the flour, sugar, baking powder, and salt and
add to egg mixture. Stir gently just until blended, adding a little more flour only if the
batter is too thin; it should still have a few lumps.

HEAT A GRIDDLE or large, heavy skillet and oil it lightly. Pour the batter onto the
griddle, using about ⅓ cup for each pancake, and cook over moderate heat until the
edges look dry and bubbles appear on top, 2 to 3 minutes. Arrange about 4 slices of
banana on top of each pancake, then turn and continue cooking until browned on the
other side, about 2 minutes longer. Serve banana side up, with maple syrup and butter
if you like.

Makes 4 to 6 servings

HARVEST MUFFINS

The White Swan Guest House, Mount Vernon, Washington

Innkeeper Peter Goldfarb serves these fragrant muffins hot from
the oven, accompanied by fresh fruit from his orchard and dark-roast coffee.
The secret to baking great muffins is to stir the batter gently, just until
ingredients are blended. Don't worry if the batter is still a bit
lumpy; overmixing will prevent it from rising properly.

2 cups all-purpose flour
½ cup rolled oats
1 tablespoon ground cinnamon
2 teaspoons baking powder
1 teaspoon baking soda
1 teaspoon powdered ginger
1 teaspoon salt
1 cup milk

1 carrot, grated (about 1 cup)
½ cup packed brown sugar
½ cup raisins
½ cup fresh cranberries, coarsely chopped
½ cup vegetable oil
1 egg
2 tablespoons molasses

PREHEAT THE OVEN to 400°F. Lightly grease a 12-cup muffin tin.

COMBINE THE FLOUR, oats, cinnamon, baking powder, baking soda, ginger, and salt
in a large bowl. In another bowl, stir together the milk, carrot, brown sugar, raisins, cranberries, oil, egg, and molasses.

ADD THE WET INGREDIENTS to the dry ingredients, stirring gently until just
blended but still a little lumpy. Pour the batter into the muffin tins, filling each to just
below the rim. Bake until a toothpick inserted in the center of a muffin comes out
clean, 15 to 18 minutes.

Makes 12 muffins

KAISERSCHMARREN
(Austrian Pancake)

Durlacher Hof, Whistler, British Columbia

In the ski country of Austria, *Kaiserschmarren* is served not only for
breakfast but also for afternoon dessert with plenty of good, strong coffee.
Legend has it that Austrian Emperor Franz Josef always tore his pancakes into small
bits before eating them, and that's how they're served at the Durlacher Hof, lightly
dusted with powdered sugar. Stewed prunes or cherries are a good accompaniment
(or try the Winter Fruit Compote on page 19).

2 cups all-purpose flour	*¼ cup sugar*
1 cup milk	*½ cup raisins*
½ cup unsalted butter	*Fresh or stewed fruit*
Pinch salt	*Powdered sugar, for sprinkling*
4 eggs, separated	

PREHEAT THE OVEN to 375°F.

STIR TOGETHER the flour and milk in a large bowl. Melt ¼ cup of the butter and
whisk it into the batter with the salt; then whisk in the egg yolks.

BEAT THE EGG WHITES with the sugar in a separate bowl until firm and glossy, then
gently fold the into the batter.

HEAT THE REMAINING ¼ cup butter in a 12-inch cast iron skillet. Carefully pour in
the batter and scatter the raisins evenly over it. Bake the pancake in the preheated oven
until puffed and golden, 20 to 25 minutes. Using two forks, tear the pancake into serving
pieces and arrange on individual plates. Spoon some fruit onto the pancake and sprinkle
powdered sugar over it. Serve immediately.

Makes 8 to 10 servings

LEMON CREAM CHEESE–STUFFED FRENCH TOAST

State Street Inn Bed & Breakfast, Hood River, Oregon

Innkeeper Amy Lee's favorite topping for this sweet, tart toast is
fresh, local strawberries, heated with a little orange juice and sugar to taste.
She also encourages people to try real maple syrup, or any of their favorite
fruit toppings. Be sure to slice the bread thick enough to allow an
additional cut down the center of each piece for the stuffing.

FILLING

8 ounces cream cheese, softened	*⅓ cup sugar*
Grated zest of 1 lemon	*1 loaf French or Italian bread*
Juice of ½ lemon	*(day-old, if possible)*

BATTER

6 eggs	*1 teaspoon vanilla extract*
2½ cups half-and-half	*½ teaspoon ground nutmeg*
⅓ cup sugar	

COMBINE THE CREAM CHEESE with the lemon zest, lemon juice, and sugar in
a small bowl. Stir with a fork until well blended. Slice the bread about 1½ inches thick.
Using a serrated knife, make a lengthwise slit in each slice, as if cutting them into two
thin slices, but leave the slices attached on three sides.

WITH A TABLE KNIFE or small spatula, spread about 1 heaping tablespoon of the filling in the pocket of each slice, then press the two halves together over the filling.

FOR THE BATTER, stir together the eggs, half-and-half, sugar, vanilla, and nutmeg in a flat, shallow dish. Preheat a lightly oiled griddle or a large, heavy skillet over medium heat.

DIP EACH BREAD SLICE in the batter, turning to coat it well. Carefully remove the slice and let the excess batter drip off. Cook the bread on the heated griddle until nicely browned and crisp, 2 to 3 minutes per side. Repeat with the remaining slices. Serve warm, with maple syrup or your favorite fruit topping.

Makes 6 to 8 servings

APPETIZERS

STEAMED CLAMS SOL DUC

Sol Duc Hot Springs, Port Angeles, Washington

Sol Duc Hot Springs chef Mike Rogers won first place at the
Clam Fest in Sequim, Washington, for his steamed clams. He uses Manila
clams; littleneck clams are another fine choice.

2 tablespoons olive oil	*¼ cup dry sherry*
2 tablespoons chopped sun-dried tomatoes	*¼ cup dry white wine*
1 tablespoon chopped garlic	*Juice of 1 lemon*
1 tablespoon chopped shallot	*3 tablespoons butter, cut in pieces and chilled*
2 pounds Manila clams, scrubbed	*1 green onion, chopped*
¼ cup hard cider	*4 slices baguette, sliced diagonally and toasted*

HAZELNUT BUTTER

3 tablespoons butter, softened	*1 tablespoon hazelnut liqueur (optional)*
¼ cup finely chopped toasted hazelnuts	

FOR THE HAZELNUT BUTTER, combine the butter, hazelnuts, and liqueur, if using,
in a small bowl. Set aside or refrigerate.

HEAT THE OIL in a large skillet over medium heat. Add the sun-dried tomatoes, garlic,
and shallot and cook for 2 minutes. Add the clams, hard cider, sherry, white wine, and
lemon juice. Cover and steam until the clams are open, 4 to 6 minutes. Discard any clams
that do not open. Add the butter to the pan and stir gently until it has melted. Transfer
the clams to individual shallow bowls, pour the sauce over them, and sprinkle each with
some of the green onion. Spread the toast slices with hazelnut butter, and serve alongside
the clams.

Makes 2 to 4 servings

FLASH-FRIED SQUID
with Herb Garlic Dip and Horseradish Gremolata

Etta's Seafood, Seattle, Washington

Flash-fried squid has been a favorite among Etta's Seafood customers
since the day the restaurant opened. "Flash-frying," says chef Tom Douglas,
"keeps squid from getting tough." To offset the intensity of the garlic sauce and
horseradish topping, try a distinctive Columbia pinot gris. Use any
leftover herb garlic dip for a zesty sandwich spread.

2 to 3 cups all-purpose flour	4 cups peanut oil (more if needed) for frying
1 tablespoon paprika	1½ pounds cleaned squid (see page 59), tubes
1 teaspoon salt	cut into rings
1 teaspoon pepper	Lemon wedges, for serving
1 teaspoon dried thyme	

HERB GARLIC DIP

1 whole egg	3 tablespoons finely chopped flat-leaf
1 egg yolk	(Italian) parsley
2 tablespoons freshly squeezed lemon juice	3 tablespoons finely chopped mixed herbs
2 tablespoons Dijon-style mustard	(such as thyme, chives, rosemary, and sage)
2 tablespoons red wine vinegar	1½ tablespoons finely chopped garlic
2 cups pure olive oil (not extra-virgin)	Salt and freshly ground black pepper

HORSERADISH GREMOLATA

2 tablespoons chopped flat-leaf	1 tablespoon freshly grated horseradish
(Italian) parsley	1½ teaspoons minced or grated lemon zest

FOR THE HERB GARLIC DIP, combine the egg and egg yolk in the work bowl of a food processor. Add the lemon juice, mustard, and vinegar and process until combined. With the motor running, add the oil through the tube, drizzling it very slowly at first. Once the mixture begins to emulsify, continue adding the oil in a steady stream. Add the parsley, herbs, and garlic and pulse to combine. Season to taste with salt and pepper.

FOR THE GREMOLATA, combine the parsley, horseradish, and lemon zest in a small bowl and stir to mix. Set aside.

IN A DEEP-FRYER or large, heavy pot, heat about 3 inches of oil to 350°F. To tell when the oil is hot enough, test it by adding one coated piece of squid; it should cook golden and tender within 2 minutes.

STIR TOGETHER the flour, paprika, salt, pepper, and thyme in a shallow dish. Pat the squid dry with paper towels, add it to the seasoned flour, and toss to coat thoroughly. Remove a handful of squid and put it in a mesh sieve, tossing to remove excess flour. Gently add the squid to the hot oil and fry until golden, about 2 minutes. Scoop out the squid and let drain on paper towels. Continue with the remaining squid, shaking off excess flour and frying in batches.

ARRANGE THE SQUID on a serving platter and scatter the gremolata over it. Serve with lemon wedges for squeezing and herb garlic dip alongside for dipping.

Makes 6 to 8 servings

CONFETTI GARDEN SALSA

Olympic Lights, Friday Harbor, Washington

At the Olympic Lights they use four different chiles in this salsa: mild, medium-hot, very hot, and super-hot. You can adjust the level of heat in this recipe by using hotter or milder chiles. The quinces they use, which come from their own trees, have a very firm, crunchy texture and lemony tart flavor. Not all quince will be suitable for this recipe—some are too coarse and tart. Lemon juice and zest make a fine substitution.

This is a case where chopping the vegetables by hand produces a more appealing texture than can be achieved with a food processor. Serve this salsa with chips or on grilled fish. It is best freshly made, but it will keep for up to 2 days covered in the refrigerator.

2 quinces, peeled, seeded, and minced, or the juice and grated zest of 1 lemon
2 large, ripe tomatoes, cored and minced
½ large Walla Walla Sweet onion, minced
1 yellow or red bell pepper, cored, seeded, and minced
½ pound broccoli, stems peeled if tough, minced
½ cup loosely packed flat-leaf (Italian) parsley, minced
½ cup loosely packed cilantro, minced
1 small carrot, minced

6 cloves garlic, minced
1 mild chile (such as Anaheim), cored, seeded, and minced
2 or 3 medium-hot chiles (such as jalapeño), cored, seeded, and minced
2 or 3 very hot chiles (such as serrano), cored, seeded, and minced (optional)
2 or 3 super-hot chiles (such as habanero or Thai bird), cored, seeded, and minced (optional)
Salt and freshly ground black pepper

COMBINE THE QUINCE, tomato, onion, bell pepper, broccoli, parsley, cilantro, carrot, garlic, and chiles in a large bowl. Toss to mix well, and season to taste with salt and pepper.

Makes about 4 cups

WALLA WALLA SWEETS

There's no doubt Northwesterners are passionate about their onions—Walla Walla Sweets, that is. From mid-June to mid-August, onion lovers flock to the small town of Walla Walla, Washington, to purchase these fragrant bulbs at roadside stands and backyard refrigerators, where you leave your money in a jar.

Celebrated all over the United States for their mild, sweet flesh, Walla Walla Sweet onions have been a favorite since the early 1900s, when they were brought to the Northwest from Italy. They are one of a handful of onion varieties that people enjoy raw, like an apple. Their flesh is sweet, crisp, and succulent without the painful sting of other onions.

Why do Walla Walla Sweets taste so sweet? It begins with the variety of seed. Soil is another important factor in determining an onion's pungency. "Our soil is a clay/mineral type that is very low in sulfur," explains Brian Magnaghi, general manager of the Walla Walla Gardeners Association.

Sulfur-based compounds and other carbohydrates give cooking onions their powerful, tear-inducing aromas, and act as natural preservatives. Walla Walla Sweets have just half the sulfur content of an ordinary yellow onion.

To qualify as genuine Walla Walla Sweets, the onions must be grown within a specific geographic area, which encompasses Walla Walla County in Southwestern Washington and a small section of Umatilla County in Northeastern Oregon. Fresh Walla Walla Sweets are available only from mid-June to mid-August.

Most growers raise their own seed, which is planted during the first two weeks of September. "Onions planted in the fall develop less of the pungent sulfur compounds and are much sweeter than onions that are spring planted," explains Magnaghi. By the time the seedlings have reached the size of a small green onion, cold weather has set in, and the onions are left in the fields to winter over.

STUFFED WALLA WALLA SWEETS

Green Gables Inn, Walla Walla, Washington

Set in the heart of Walla Walla Sweet onion country, the Green Gables
Inn serves these stuffed onion appetizers bubbling over with a savory filling
of sausage, bread crumbs, and cheddar cheese. Jumbo-sized onions can be served as
a main course. The juicy sweetness of Walla Walla Sweets is always enhanced by a
sweet, velvety red wine brimming with dark cherry and black currant
flavors, such as a Leonetti Cellar merlot.

4 medium Walla Walla Sweet onions (10 to 12 ounces each)	2 tablespoons chopped flat-leaf (Italian) parsley
⅔ pound bulk pork sausage	½ teaspoon sugar
¾ cup bread crumbs	¼ teaspoon ground cinnamon
⅓ cup grated cheddar cheese	Salt and freshly ground black pepper
1 egg, lightly beaten	1 slice bacon, cut in 4 pieces (optional)
3 tablespoons milk	

PEEL THE ONIONS and cut ½ inch off the top and bottom of each one. Bring a
large pan of water to a boil, add the onions, and boil for 7 minutes. Drain the onions
and let cool slightly. When cool enough to handle, remove the centers from the onions,
leaving a shell of at least 3 layers. Reserve the onion centers for the stuffing. If you cannot easily push out an onion center, use a spoon to scoop out some of the flesh until
the center comes free, or cut out the center with a small knife. If a shell splits, wrap a
thin strip of foil around the onion to hold it together. Set the onion shells in a lightly
greased baking dish.

PREHEAT THE OVEN to 350°F.

FRY THE SAUSAGE in a skillet over medium heat until no pink remains, about 10 minutes, breaking it into small pieces as it cooks. Drain well, discarding the fat.

FINELY CHOP enough of the reserved onion centers to make 2 cups. In a large bowl, combine the onion, sausage, bread crumbs, cheese, egg, milk, parsley, sugar, and cinnamon with a pinch each of salt and pepper. Mix well and stuff the mixture into the onion shells. Top each with a piece of bacon, if desired, and bake until the stuffing is very hot and the onion is tender, 30 to 40 minutes.

Makes 4 servings

TO STORE WALLA WALLA SWEETS

The best place to store Walla Walla Sweets is in the refrigerator. Stored in this way, they will often keep through Thanksgiving or even Christmas. For shorter-term storage, try panty hose or mesh bags, which keep air circulating around the onions. Simply put the onions, one at a time, into the legs of panty hose, tying a knot above each one. To use, snip below the lowest knot. Hung in a cool, ventilated location, Walla Walla Sweets will keep for 3 to 6 weeks.

PEPPER-CURED SMOKED SALMON

Stonehedge Inn, Hood River, Oregon

This spicy smoked salmon is marinated in a fragrant brine flavored
with garlic, white wine, juniper berries, cardamom, and black pepper, then
delicately smoked over hardwood. The chefs at the Stonehedge Inn swear
by their Little Chief Smoker, which is made by the local Hood River–based Luhr
Jensen company, but you can use an electric or charcoal smoker. The sauce
verte is best made at least a few hours in advance.

For the Little Chief Smoker, very fine chips of wood (alder is a favorite)
are used dry, and the electric heat source maintains a very low temperature,
so 2 to 3 hours may be needed to smoke a fillet of fish (and chips may need
replenishing during that time). For charcoal-heated smokers, larger chunks of wood
chips are used and they are usually soaked in water before adding to the coals,
so the chips produce more smoke for a longer time. Depending on the heat
of the charcoal smoker, the fish can be smoked in 1 to 2 hours.

2 cups warm water	1 tablespoon juniper berries, lightly crushed
1½ cups white wine	1 teaspoon thyme leaves
1 cup packed light brown sugar	2 to 3 pounds salmon fillets, skin and
½ cup kosher salt	pin bones removed
1 tablespoon chopped garlic	3 to 4 tablespoons cracked black peppercorns
1 tablespoon whole green cardamom pods,	
lightly crushed	

SAUCE VERTE

2 cups mayonnaise	1 tablespoon minced chives
3 tablespoons minced cilantro	1 tablespoon minced tarragon
3 tablespoons minced flat-leaf (Italian) parsley	1 clove garlic, minced
2 tablespoons honey	Splash freshly squeezed lemon juice
2 tablespoons stone-ground mustard	

COMBINE THE WARM WATER, wine, brown sugar, salt, garlic, cardamom, juniper berries, and thyme in a 9- by 13-inch baking dish and stir until the sugar and salt have dissolved. Let cool completely.

CUT THE SALMON into 4-ounce pieces and set them in the brine. Let cure in the refrigerator for 6 to 8 hours.

FOR THE SAUCE VERTE, combine the mayonaise, cilantro, parsley, honey, mustard, chives, tarragon, garlic, and lemon juice and whisk to mix well. Refrigerate until needed.

PREHEAT THE SMOKER according to the manufacturer's directions; if necessary, soak the smoking chips.

REMOVE THE SALMON from the brine, discarding the brine. Rinse the fish and dry it well with paper towels. Sprinkle the salmon pieces liberally with cracked black pepper, pressing the peppercorns gently to help them adhere to the fish. Arrange the salmon on the racks in the smoker and gently smoke for 1 to 3 hours, depending on the type of smoker used. The salmon will form a skin and will lightly crack when pressed with a finger, but will still be tender and moist at the center.

LET THE SALMON COOL and serve it with the sauce verte on the side.

Makes 8 to 12 servings

DUNGENESS CRAB WONTONS
with Thai Dipping Sauce

Bay House, Lincoln City, Oregon

Filled with sweet Dungeness crab and minced vegetables, these
fragrant wontons are dipped in a spicy sauce flavored with hot chile oil and
Thai fish sauce. If you can't find Thai fish sauce in the specialty food section of
your local market, soy sauce can be substituted. Wonton skins are available in the
produce section of many supermarkets. When making the wontons, be sure to
squeeze excess liquid from the crab and chopped vegetable mixture. For a change
of pace, you can pan-fry the wontons rather than simmering them.
Pair them with a crisp, spicy Oregon pinot gris.

16 wonton skins	Black sesame seeds, for garnish (optional)
1 egg	Cilantro sprigs, for garnish
2 tablespoons cold water	

FILLING

4 ounces Dungeness crabmeat	1 tablespoon minced red bell pepper
½ cup chopped napa cabbage	1 tablespoon minced green bell pepper
¼ cup chopped bok choy	1 tablespoon minced ginger
2 tablespoons grated carrot	1 tablespoon minced cilantro
1 tablespoon minced green onion	

THAI DIPPING SAUCE

½ cup seasoned rice wine vinegar	1½ teaspoons hot chile oil, or to taste
1½ teaspoons Thai fish sauce (nam pla)	

FOR THE FILLING, pick over the crabmeat to remove any bits of shell or cartilage, then squeeze the crabmeat to remove excess moisture. Combine the cabbage, bok choy, carrot, green onion, red and green pepper, ginger, and cilantro in a food processor and pulse to finely chop and thoroughly mix, 3 to 4 pulses. Squeeze the chopped vegetables to remove excess moisture. Put the vegetables in a bowl with the crab and toss to mix well.

FOR THE THAI DIPPING SAUCE, stir together the vinegar and fish sauce in a small bowl. Add hot chile oil to taste and set aside.

LAY THE WONTON SKINS on a lightly floured work surface. Whisk together the egg and water in a small bowl. Put a scant tablespoon of the crab filling in the center of each wonton skin. Lightly brush the edges with the egg mixture and fold the edges over to form triangles, pressing the edges well to seal.

BRING A LARGE PAN of water to a boil and lower the heat to a simmer. Add the wontons, a few at a time, and cook in the simmering water until just tender, 2 to 3 minutes. Scoop them out with a slotted spoon and drain well. Arrange the drained wontons on a serving platter with a small bowl of Thai dipping sauce. Sprinkle the black sesame seeds over them, garnish with sprigs of cilantro, and serve immediately.

Makes 4 servings

SAMSA
(Uzbekistan Lamb-Filled Pastries)

The Kaleenka, Seattle, Washington

Filled with cumin-spiced ground lamb, these flaky pastries are dipped in a
snappy green sauce flavored with parsley, cucumber, fresh dill, and garlic. The sauce
also makes a great dressing for salads or steamed vegetables.

¾ pound ground lamb	*1 teaspoon salt*
1 medium onion, finely chopped	*½ teaspoon freshly ground black pepper*
1½ tablespoons whole cumin seed	

DOUGH

4 cups all-purpose flour, more if needed	*1 teaspoon salt*
2 cups warm water	*2 tablespoons butter, softened*
2 eggs	*1 to 2 tablespoons poppy seeds, for garnish*

KALEENKA GREEN SAUCE

1 cup loosely packed flat-leaf (Italian) parsley	*1 cup oil*
4 green onions, trimmed and coarsely chopped	*½ cup freshly squeezed lemon juice*
1 large or 2 small stalks celery, trimmed and coarsely chopped	*2 or 3 cloves garlic*
	½ teaspoon salt
½ cucumber, coarsely chopped	*½ teaspoon sugar*
2 tablespoons chopped dill	

TO MAKE THE KALEENKA GREEN SAUCE, purée the parsley, green onions,
celery, cucumber, and dill in a food processor or blender. Add the oil, lemon juice, garlic,
salt, and sugar and process until light and creamy. Refrigerate until needed.

COMBINE THE LAMB, onion, cumin, salt, and pepper in a large bowl. Stir to mix well; set aside.

FOR THE DOUGH, combine the flour, warm water, one of the eggs, and the salt in the large bowl of an electric mixer. Mix until blended, then beat in the butter. Continue mixing until a soft but not sticky dough is formed, adding more flour if necessary. Knead the dough for a few minutes, cover with a towel or plastic wrap, and let rest 10 to 15 minutes.

PREHEAT THE OVEN to 350°F.

CUT THE DOUGH into quarters. Place one of the pieces on a floured surface and roll out to a thickness of ¼ inch. Cut the dough into rounds about 4 inches in diameter. Place 1 rounded tablespoon of filling in the center of each dough circle. Fold the dough over the filling and pinch the edges to seal and completely enclose the filling. Set on a greased baking sheet with the pinched side down. Repeat with the remaining dough and filling.

BEAT THE REMAINING EGG with ¼ cup water and brush lightly over the samsa. Sprinkle the poppy seeds over them and bake until lightly browned, 25 to 30 minutes. Arrange the samsa on a large platter, with the Kaleenka green sauce alongside.

Makes 4 servings, about 20 pastries

GARLIC AND THYME CRÈME BRÛLÉE

with Chive Cornmeal Crackers

Oceanwood Country Inn, Mayne Island, British Columbia

Flavored with mashed, roasted garlic and fresh thyme, these pungent custards can be served alone or spread on homemade chive cornmeal crackers. The chefs at Oceanwood Country Inn use a template to form these crackers, but you could just as easily do them freehand, spreading batter into thin shapes.

2 whole heads garlic	*1¼ cups whipping cream*
2 teaspoons olive oil	*1 tablespoon minced thyme*
1 sprig thyme	*Salt and freshly ground black pepper*
6 egg yolks	

CHIVE CORNMEAL CRACKERS

²/₃ cup all-purpose flour	*¼ teaspoon baking powder*
¼ cup yellow cornmeal	*½ cup milk, more if needed*
1 teaspoon salt	*2 tablespoons minced chives*

PREHEAT THE OVEN to 375°F.

CUT A RECTANGLE about 2 inches wide and 4 inches long from the middle of a sturdy piece of thin cardboard or a disposable plastic lid. This will be a template for forming the crackers.

FOR THE CRACKERS, stir together the flour, cornmeal, salt, and baking powder. Stir in the milk. The batter should be smooth and spreadable; add a little more milk if needed. Stir in the chives. Set the template on a lightly greased or parchment-lined baking sheet. With a spatula, spread the batter inside the template to form a thin rectangle, then lift off the template. Repeat with the remaining batter; you will need to bake the crackers in batches. Bake the crackers until crisp, about 12 minutes. Carefully transfer the crackers to a wire rack to cool. Repeat with the remaining batter. Keep the oven set at 375°F.

PUT THE GARLIC HEADS on a square of foil, drizzle the olive oil over them, and set the sprig of thyme alongside the garlic. Wrap the foil snugly around the garlic and bake until soft, about 30 minutes. When cool enough to handle, peel the individual cloves of garlic and lightly mash them in a bowl. Distribute the garlic evenly among six ½-cup ramekins. Reduce the oven temperature to 300°F.

BEAT THE EGG YOLKS with the cream until well blended, then stir in the minced thyme with a pinch each of salt and pepper. Pour the mixture over the garlic in the ramekins and set them in a large baking pan. Add hot water to the baking pan so that it comes about halfway up the sides of the ramekins. Cover the dish with foil and bake the custards until they have just set, about 40 to 50 minutes. Remove the ramekins from the water and set aside to cool. Serve at room temperature, with the crackers on the side.

Makes 6 servings

SALMON BELLY TEMPURA

Waterfront Centre Hotel, Vancouver, British Columbia

Salmon bellies are the fattiest and most succulent portion of salmon.
You can substitute strips of fatty king or sockeye salmon. Kombu is a Japanese
seaweed, available dried in specialty Asian markets. Any of the eight species of edible
Northwest kelp can be substituted. All kelps are rich in vitamins, minerals, and
protein. Dried bonito flakes are made from a small species of Japanese
fish that is dried, smoked, and fermented.

1 pound salmon belly, skinned and cut into
12 strips (each about 2 by 4 by ½ inches)
1½ cups tempura batter mix,
plus more for dredging salmon

2 cups ice water
2 egg yolks
Vegetable oil, for frying

TENJU DIPPING SAUCE

1 cup water
1 ounce kombu (dried kelp)
½ ounce dried bonito flakes (about ½ cup)

½ cup soy sauce
½ cup mirin or dry sherry

FOR THE DIPPING SAUCE, combine the water and kombu in a small saucepan,
bring to a boil, and simmer for 1 minute. Add the bonito flakes and simmer 1 minute
longer. Stir in the soy sauce and mirin and simmer for 1 more minute. Strain the sauce
into a bowl and keep warm.

FOR THE TEMPURA, thread each salmon strip onto the top portion of a 6- to 8-inch bamboo skewer, leaving the bottom end free for easy handling. Dredge the salmon in some of the dry tempura batter mix, patting to remove any excess.

HEAT 2 TO 3 INCHES of oil to 350°F over medium heat in a large, deep, heavy pan; the oil should come no more than halfway up the sides of the pan.

WHILE THE OIL is heating, stir together the water and egg yolks in a medium bowl. Add the 1½ cups tempura flour and stir lightly just until mixed; the batter should still be a little lumpy. Dip 2 or 3 of the salmon skewers into the batter, allowing excess to drip off. Gently place the skewers in the hot oil and fry until the batter is lightly golden and the salmon is just cooked through, 1 to 2 minutes. Repeat with the remaining skewers.

ARRANGE THE SKEWERS on a platter or individual plates, with bowls of the warm dipping sauce on the side.

Makes 4 to 6 servings

ITALIAN BAKED OYSTERS

Cafe Luna, Shelton, Washington

Home to the annual Skookum Rotary Oysterfest held each October,
Shelton, Washington, is one town that definitely loves its oysters. This dish is
perfect for a dinner party, since you can prepare it in advance and refrigerate it
until you are ready to bake and serve. Instead of using individual baking dishes, you
can bake the oysters in one large dish and divide them among individual plates
for serving. For a delicious match, serve these oysters with
Columbia Winery's Chevrier Semillon Sur Lie.

*24 extra-small oysters, shucked,
or two 10-ounce jars
¼ cup extra-virgin olive oil
2 tablespoons butter
⅔ cup bread crumbs
2 tablespoons minced green onion*

*2 tablespoons minced flat-leaf (Italian) parsley
1 tablespoon minced tarragon
1 tablespoon minced garlic
Pinch cayenne
Salt and freshly ground black pepper*

PREHEAT THE OVEN to 450°F.

DIVIDE THE OYSTERS among 4 individual gratin dishes. Combine the olive oil
and butter in a small pan and gently heat just until the butter has melted. In a separate
bowl, combine the bread crumbs, green onion, parsley, tarragon, garlic, and cayenne with
salt and pepper to taste. Pour the olive oil/butter mixture over the crumbs and stir to
mix well.

SPRINKLE THE TOPPING over the oysters and set the dishes on a baking sheet for
easy handling. Bake the oysters until the crumbs are lightly browned and the oysters are
plump, 12 to 15 minutes.

Makes 4 servings

Few foods evoke more passion among their eaters than oysters—due no doubt in part to their reputation as the ultimate aphrodisiac. Passion aside, oysters are low in calories and high in vitamins and minerals, containing large amounts of zinc, phosphorus, iron, copper, and iodine.

Recently the Pacific Northwest surpassed the Gulf Coast region to become the top oyster-producing region in the United States. Interestingly, only one variety of oyster is indigenous to the Pacific Northwest—the tiny, coppery-flavored Olympia oyster. During the mid- to late 1800s, this oyster was in such great demand that enormous quantities from Willapa Bay and Samish Bay were shipped to restaurants in San Francisco. By the early 1900s, Olympia oysters were nearly extinct due to overharvesting and pollution. Fortunately, several Northwest companies have successfully revived the Olympia oyster industry.

Pacific oysters (native to China and Japan) are the main oyster of commerce in the Northwest today. The Kumamoto is a small variety of Pacific oyster. Local growers raise several other species of oyster, including the European flat oyster. Westcott flats, raised by Westcott Bay Sea Farms on San Juan Island, are a prime example of this species.

Oysters raised in the Northwest are often named for the area in which they are grown: Quilcene, Oysterville Specials, Hamma Hamma, Snow Creek, Skookum, Goose Point, and Fanny Bay oysters (all Pacific oysters). Like wines, oysters develop unique flavors and qualities, depending on their variety and where they grow. The salinity of the water, the presence of algae or eel grass in the growing beds and the amount of rainfall all affect an oyster's color, shape, and flavor. Different growing methods (bottom culture, raft or tray culture, and dike culture) also contribute to an oyster's flavor and texture.

During the spawning season, triggered by summer heat, oysters consume their stores of glycogen (a sweet-tasting starch), giving them energy to produce both sperm and eggs. The byproduct of this glycogen consumption is lactic acid, which gives the oysters a milky appearance and a less assertive flavor. Consequently, many people prefer to eat oysters only in cooler months, or any month with an "R" as the old adage goes.

Note: People with depressed immune systems, liver diseases, AIDS, cancer, or alcoholism should avoid eating raw oysters.

WARM SALMON SPREAD

Mount Ashland Inn, Ashland, Oregon

At the Mount Ashland Inn they use jars of home-smoked salmon in this horseradish-spiked spread. Use your favorite hot-smoked salmon for this easy-to-prepare appetizer. Serve with breads and crackers or with fresh vegetables.

8 ounces hot-smoked salmon, skin and bones removed
8 ounces cream cheese, softened
2 tablespoons minced sweet onion

1 tablespoon milk
1 tablespoon prepared horseradish
Salt and freshly ground black pepper
⅓ cup slivered almonds

PREHEAT THE OVEN to 375°F.

STIR TOGETHER the smoked salmon, cream cheese, onion, milk, and horseradish in a medium bowl. Add salt and pepper to taste. When well blended, put the mixture in a small baking dish, preferably one suitable for serving. Sprinkle the almonds on top and bake until the mixture is bubbly and the almonds are lightly browned, 12 to 15 minutes. Serve warm with crackers, bread slices, or vegetables.

Makes 4 to 6 servings

When buying smoked fish, look for flesh that glows, like fresh fish. It should smell sweet and clean like the sea, with a subtle balance of natural alder (or other hardwood) smoke flavor. Avoid smoked salmon that has been dyed red, fish that lists liquid smoke as an ingredient, or any fish that smells "fishy."

Hot smoked: Seafood that has been cooked, after being smoked, to an internal temperature of 145°F. The seafood is first cured in salt or brine; then it is drained, dried, smoked, cooked, and cooled. Hot-smoked salmon is moist, firm, and meaty, with the buttery texture and earthy sweetness prized by salmon connoisseurs. When recipes call for smoked salmon as an ingredient, hot-smoked salmon is preferred.

Cold smoked: Seafood that has been smoked but not cooked, with internal temperatures reaching no higher than 85°F. In the cold-smoking process, seafood is first dry-cured; then it is smoked and cooled. Silky and tender, slices of cold-smoked seafood melt on the palate with a velvety softness and a buttery finish. Cold-smoked salmon, and salmon cured by other means, are best enjoyed as is.

Nova: The term "Nova" refers to Nova Scotia, where many New York fish smokers used to buy their salmon. This cold-smoked salmon is typically less salty than lox.

Lox: Salmon that has been cured in a salty brine for up to a year and sometimes, but rarely, lightly smoked.

Kippered: Traditionally a British product, kippers are cold-smoked, split fat herring. In the United States, "kippered" (also known as "Northwest-style") usually refers to hot-smoked seafood with a high moisture content.

Gravlax: Uncooked salmon that has been cured in a mixture of salt, sugar, pepper, dill, and sometimes distilled spirits (not smoked). In Scandinavia, gravlax was traditionally buried in the earth to cure (sometimes for over a year), hence the name *grav*, meaning "grave."

Dried (jerky): Sometimes called "Indian hard-cure salmon," this is salmon that has been cured and then dried (sometimes by smoking).

CALAMARI NEAPOLITAN STYLE

Roberto's Restaurant, Friday Harbor, Washington

When a prep cook at Roberto's mistakenly plumped a huge quantity of raisins, the chef devised a creative use for them. This unusual appetizer has since become a house favorite. Squid cooks very quickly (just a couple of minutes in a hot pan), so be sure to have all the other ingredients ready beforehand. An elegant dry gewürztraminer is a delicious match for this dish.

1 pound cleaned squid tubes, cut in 1-inch rings and patted dry
½ cup all-purpose flour
2 tablespoons olive oil
⅓ cup raisins, soaked in ½ cup warm water until plump

⅓ cup toasted pine nuts
2 tablespoons minced garlic
1 cup chopped plum (Roma) tomatoes
¼ cup chopped flat-leaf (Italian) parsley
Juice of 1 lemon
Lemon wedges, for serving

COMBINE THE SQUID RINGS and flour in a small bag, hold the top closed, and toss to coat the squid in the flour. Remove the squid from the bag, shake off the excess flour, and set aside on a plate.

HEAT THE OLIVE OIL in a large, heavy skillet over medium-high heat. When hot, add the squid and cook for 1 minute. Drain the plumped raisins, discarding the water, and add them to the squid with the pine nuts and garlic. Cook for 1 minute longer, then stir in the tomatoes, parsley, and lemon juice.

SPOON THE SQUID and sauce onto individual plates and serve immediately, with bread or rolls on the side.

Makes 4 servings

SQUID

There are many species of squid (also known as calamari or ink-fish), but the main one sold commercially in the Northwest is *Loligo opalescens*, named for its opalescent flesh. The tender, cigar-shaped body of a squid is equipped with a strong beak for cutting up its feed and an internal skeleton (called a quill or pen). Ten long tentacles are attached just above its eyes. Squid also have an ink sac, from which they squirt a dark, inky (but edible) liquid to confuse and scare off predators.

Squid used in cooking are usually just 5 to 8 inches long. Once cleaned, these small squid can be sliced into rings or left whole and stuffed. Meat from larger squid is sometimes marketed as steaks; tenderize these before cooking by pounding them paper-thin with a mallet.

On the West Coast, fresh squid is available in early summer and late winter. When buying squid, look for sweet-smelling specimens with bright, shiny skin. The color should be white and purple, with no brown spots. Cleaned squid freezes well if carefully wrapped. Squid cooks quickly, becoming tough when overcooked. To prevent overcooking, test it repeatedly while cooking, carefully biting into a piece to see that it's opaque through but tender. Remove squid from the heat the instant it is done. Two pounds of whole squid will yield one and a half pounds of cleaned squid.

Cleaning squid is a very simple process but is not for the squeamish.

1. Using your fingers, peel off the mottled purple skin. Don't worry if some stubborn patches remain.
2. Pull out the head by inserting your thumb and one or two fingers into the body, below the point where the head is attached. Together with the head, pull out as many innards as possible.
3. Reach into the body and pull out the quill and any remaining innards. Use a spoon or knife to clean the body more thoroughly.
4. Rinse out the body cavity (the "tube") under cold running water. Blot dry.
5. Using a sharp knife, sever the tentacles from the head just above the beak (the hard ball located just above the squid's eyes). Reserve the edible tentacles and discard the head, beak, and innards.
6. Refrigerate cleaned squid on ice, and use within 24 hours.

ALDER-GRILLED FANNY BAY OYSTERS

Salmon House on the Hill, Vancouver, British Columbia

In this recipe chef Dan Atkinson infuses local Fanny Bay oysters and native oyster mushrooms with the complex flavor of alder smoke. Hot from the grill, the oysters and mushrooms are drizzled with a flavorful herb vinaigrette.

3 thick slices bacon, preferably alder-smoked	*¼ cup minced red bell pepper*
¼ cup malt vinegar	*¼ cup minced red onion*
2 tablespoons minced mixed herbs (such as basil, thyme, parsley, dill, and cilantro)	*1 jalapeño pepper, cored, seeded, ribs removed, and very finely minced*
1 clove garlic	*1 teaspoon cracked black pepper*
1 teaspoon sugar	*12 medium or 24 small Fanny Bay oysters in the shell*
1 teaspoon whole-grain mustard	*½ pound oyster mushrooms, trimmed and cleaned*
Pinch salt	
½ cup olive oil	

PREHEAT an outdoor grill and soak 2 handfuls of alder chips in a bowl of water.

COOK THE BACON PIECES over the hot coals until crisp, 3 to 5 minutes. Drain well on paper towels and then cut into ¼-inch pieces and set aside. Combine the vinegar, herbs, garlic, sugar, mustard, and salt in a blender or food processor. Blend for 1 minute, then slowly add the olive oil, scraping down the sides as needed. When the oil is fully incorporated, pour the mixture into a bowl and stir in the bacon, bell pepper, onion, jalapeño, and black pepper. Set aside.

WHEN THE GRILL is hot, drain the wood chips well and scatter them over the coals. Set the oysters, cupped side down, on the grate, with the oyster mushrooms alongside them. Cover the grill and cook just until the oysters pop open and the mushrooms are tender, 3 to 5 minutes. Discard the top shells. Arrange the oysters and the mushrooms on individual plates. Drizzle with some of the vinaigrette, passing the rest separately. Serve immediately.

Makes 4 servings

When buying oysters, look for ones with shells that are tightly closed or that close readily when tapped (that means they're alive). The meat should be tan to cream-colored, heavy and plump, with a sweet sea odor.

Store live oysters at between 34° and 40°F. Place them flat side up in an open container and cover with a damp towel. Oysters stored this way will keep from four to seven days. Freshly shucked oyster meats should be packed in their own juices (known as the oyster's liquor), which should be clear. Stored at 34° to 40°F, these will keep up to one week. Jarred, shucked, locally produced oysters are great for stewing, pan-frying, or baking.

To shuck oysters, the first thing you need is a good oyster knife. Many different styles are available, with short, medium, or long blades. Choose a knife that feels comfortable in your hand and that has a stainless steel blade.

1. If you will be serving the oysters raw or on the half shell, begin by preparing a plate with a bed of crushed ice to hold the opened oysters.

2. Clean the oysters thoroughly under cold running water, using a stiff brush to remove any dirt.

3. Using a folded kitchen towel to protect your hand, either cup the oyster in your hand or place it on the counter with its cupped shell down to catch the juices.

4. Using your other hand, wedge the tip of the oyster knife into the hinge of the oyster, pushing and twisting until the hinge pops.

5. Sever the adductor muscle from the top shell by sliding the oyster knife as close as possible along the inside of the upper shell.

6. Pry off the top shell.

7. Loosen the oyster from the bottom shell by running the knife under the oyster, as close as possible to the shell, and severing the bottom adductor muscle. Retain as much liquor as possible.

8. Set the shucked oysters on the crushed ice or store as described above.

SPICY SINGAPORE PRAWNS

Kasteel Franssen, Oak Harbor, Washington

Served on a bed of sweet-and-sour bean thread noodles, these
fragrant prawns are spiced with hot red pepper flakes, garlic, and cilantro. The heat
of this dish calls out for a spicy Northwest riesling with a hint of sweetness,
such as a Paul Thomas dry riesling.

1 package (3½ ounces) bean thread noodles	*2 tablespoons minced garlic*
1¼ cups rice wine vinegar	*2 tablespoons chopped green onion*
1 cup sugar	*1 tablespoon chopped cilantro*
1 cup water	*2 to 3 teaspoons dried red pepper flakes*
1 tablespoon peanut or vegetable oil	*¼ cup white wine*
20 large shrimp (about 1 pound),	*1 tablespoon soy sauce*
peeled and deveined	*½ cup butter, cut in pieces and chilled*

BRING A LARGE PAN of water to a boil, add the bean thread noodles, and cook until
tender, about 5 minutes. Meanwhile, combine 1 cup of the vinegar with the sugar and
water in a large bowl and stir until the sugar is dissolved. Drain the cooked noodles, add
them to the vinegar mixture, and toss to coat well. Set aside to marinate; keep warm.

HEAT THE OIL in a large skillet over high heat. Add the shrimp and cook for about 1
minute, then stir in the garlic, green onion, cilantro, and red pepper flakes. Add the wine,
the remaining ¼ cup of rice wine vinegar, and the soy sauce and bring just to a boil. Add
the butter pieces and stir to slowly incorporate into the sauce. Remove from the heat
and taste for seasoning, adding more soy sauce or red pepper flakes to taste.

DRAIN THE WARM NOODLES, discarding the marinade, and divide them among
4 shallow bowls. Arrange the shrimp on the noodles, spoon the sauce over them, and
serve immediately.

Makes 4 servings

SHIITAKE MUSHROOM PÂTÉ

Sylvia Beach Hotel, Newport, Oregon

At the Sylvia Beach Hotel they serve this earthy pâté with Dijon mustard and homemade bread or crackers. A glass of Oregon pinot noir is a delicious accompaniment. You can substitute regular button mushrooms for half of the shiitakes.

8 ounces cream cheese, softened

½ cup sour cream

¼ cup grated Parmesan cheese

3 eggs

1 cup soft bread crumbs

2 pounds shiitake mushrooms, cleaned, trimmed, and halved

½ large onion, coarsely chopped

1 tablespoon minced garlic

2 tablespoons dried basil

1 tablespoon dried thyme

1½ teaspoons dried oregano

1½ teaspoons dried rosemary

Salt

PREHEAT THE OVEN to 350°F.

COMBINE THE CREAM CHEESE, sour cream, Parmesan cheese, and eggs in a food processor and process until smooth. Put the bread crumbs in a large bowl and pour the cream cheese mixture over them. Process the mushrooms, onion, and garlic in the food processor, pulsing until they are evenly chopped; you may need to work in batches. Do not overprocess; the mushroom mixture should still be somewhat chunky. Add it to the cream cheese mixture, followed by the basil, thyme, oregano, and rosemary. Stir to mix well, adding a pinch of salt.

GENEROUSLY GREASE a 9-inch springform pan. Line the bottom with a round of parchment paper and grease the paper. Press the mushroom mixture evenly into the prepared pan, pressing it down evenly. Top with a greased round of parchment paper, then cover the pan with foil. Bake until a knife blade inserted in the center for a few seconds comes out hot, about 1 hour. Serve either warm or chilled, cut into wedges.

Makes 12 to 16 servings

CRAB AND AVOCADO HOPPA ROLLS

Raku Kushiyaki, Vancouver, British Columbia

The California sushi roll and an Indonesian curry dish served in bowl-shaped
coconut pancakes (called "hoppers") inspired these hoppa rolls. Pickled ginger can
be found in specialty food sections, along with canned coconut milk.

1 cup crabmeat (about 6 ounces)	*2 cups mixed greens, rinsed and dried*
½ cup loosely packed basil leaves,	*1 ripe avocado, peeled, pitted, and*
preferably Thai basil	*thinly sliced*

HOPPA CREPES

⅔ cup rice flour	*5 eggs*
½ cup all-purpose flour	*Pinch salt*
1 can (14 ounces) unsweetened coconut milk	*1 to 2 teaspoons vegetable oil, for*
½ cup milk	*frying crepes*

GINGER VINAIGRETTE

⅓ cup vegetable oil	*1 clove garlic*
⅓ cup loosely packed cilantro leaves	*½ teaspoon red chile garlic paste*
¼ cup pickled ginger	*(such as* sambal badjak *or* sambal oelek)*
½ tablespoon minced fresh ginger	*½ teaspoon cider vinegar*
1 serrano chile, halved, cored, and seeded	

FOR THE CREPES, stir together the rice flour and the all-purpose flour in a
medium bowl. Add the coconut milk, regular milk, eggs, and salt and gently whisk
until thoroughly blended.

HEAT ½ TEASPOON of the vegetable oil in a crepe pan or medium skillet. Add about ¼ cup of the batter, tilting and turning the pan so it evenly coats the bottom. Cook over medium heat until the edges are lightly browned, 1 to 2 minutes. Flip the crepe and cook until the second side is lightly browned, about 1 minute longer.

REPEAT WITH THE REMAINING batter, adding more oil as needed. Layer the crepes between pieces of plastic wrap or waxed paper. You will need 6 to 8 good crepes; don't worry if you have to discard the first one or two.

FOR THE VINAIGRETTE, combine the oil, cilantro, pickled ginger, fresh ginger, chile, garlic, chile paste, and vinegar in a food processor or blender and process until smooth. Taste for seasoning and set aside.

TO ASSEMBLE THE ROLLS, lay one of the crepes on the work surface and arrange a few basil leaves across the center of the crepe. Top with a row of the greens, followed by a few teaspoons of the ginger vinaigrette. Arrange some of the crabmeat over the greens, and set a couple of slices of avocado on top. Roll the crepe up in a cylinder around the filling. Repeat with the remaining crepes and serve.

Makes 6 to 8 servings

MATCHING NORTHWEST WINES AND FOODS

Outstanding food and wine matches usually involve a combination of contrasts and similarities. Here in the Pacific Northwest, certain pairings of regional foods and wines are quickly becoming classics. Magic happens when you combine an earthy pinot noir, packed with flavors of fresh berries and spice, with the buttery-rich flavor of salmon. Another popular combination is cracked Dungeness crab and dry riesling; the crab is superbly matched by the wine's crisp, refreshing fruit and tangy mineral flavors.

By experimenting, you can invent a classic pairing of your own. Match a rich, velvety merlot with tender, Northwest lamb. Enjoy a crisp, herbaceous semillon with local goat cheese. Pair pinot gris with mussels and vegetarian dishes. Or serve nectar-sweet late harvest wines with Oregon blue cheese, toasted hazelnuts, and apple desserts.

STEAMED MEDITERRANEAN MUSSELS

Inn at Ludlow Bay, Port Ludlow, Washington

A creamy, summery sauce flavored with coconut milk, lemongrass, garlic, and cilantro highlights the sweet flavor of plump Mediterranean mussels, which are in their prime during the summer months. If you are counting calories, reduce the amount of butter called for, or leave it out entirely. If you have trouble finding lemongrass, you can use slices of lemon in its place. Look for a crisp, refreshing wine with lots of lemony acids and bold fruit flavors, such as Columbia Crest's lively semillon-chardonnay.

2 stalks lemongrass, white part only

1 plum (Roma) tomato, cored and diced

1 cup chicken stock

1 cup unsweetened coconut milk

1 tablespoon minced shallot

1 tablespoon minced cilantro

2 teaspoons minced garlic

4 pounds Mediterranean mussels, cleaned and debearded

½ cup butter, cut in pieces and chilled

Salt and freshly ground black pepper

FINELY CHOP one of the stalks of lemongrass; thinly slice the second stalk diagonally. Put the lemongrass in a large pot with the tomato, chicken stock, coconut milk, shallot, cilantro, and garlic and bring just to a boil. Add the mussels, cover the pot, and cook over medium-high heat until the mussels begin to open, about 3 minutes. Transfer the opened mussels to a large bowl and continue cooking the rest until they have opened, 2 to 3 minutes longer. Discard any mussels that do not open.

BRING THE COOKING LIQUID to a boil, and boil until reduced by about half. Add the chilled butter and stir over medium heat until it gently melts into the sauce. Remove the pan from the heat and taste the sauce for seasoning.

ARRANGE THE MUSSELS in individual shallow bowls, pour the sauce over them, and serve immediately.

Makes 4 servings

SALMON GRAVLAX

Waterfront Centre Hotel, Vancouver, British Columbia

Traditionally gravlax is served with ice-cold shots of vodka or aquavit.
Clear Creek Distillery's pear brandy is a delicious Northwest match, especially
if it's used as the brandy in the brine recipe. Be aware that this salmon
needs to cure for 48 hours in the refrigerator.

1 whole salmon fillet (about 3 pounds),	*½ cup sugar*
skin on, pin bones removed	*¼ cup brandy*
3 cups coarsely chopped dill (about 3 bunches)	*¼ cup vegetable oil*
1 cup rock salt	*2 tablespoons cracked white peppercorns*

HONEY MUSTARD DRESSING

⅓ cup white wine vinegar	*1 teaspoon minced shallot*
1 tablespoon honey, preferably unpasteurized	*¼ teaspoon minced garlic*
1 teaspoon Dijon-style grainy mustard	*1 cup vegetable oil*

SET THE SALMON, skin side down, on a rimmed tray or baking sheet. Stir together
the dill, salt, sugar, brandy, oil, and pepper. Spread the mixture over the salmon, packing
it down gently. Cover the salmon with plastic wrap and refrigerate for 48 hours.

FOR THE DRESSING, in a small bowl, whisk together the vinegar, honey, mustard,
shallot, and garlic with 1 teaspoon of the marinade from the gravlax. Whisk in the oil,
then refrigerate until needed.

JUST BEFORE SERVING, brush the dill mixture off the fish and cut the salmon into
very thin slices. Arrange the salmon slices on a serving platter or individual plates. Drizzle
some of the honey mustard dressing over it, serving the rest separately.

Makes 10 to 12 servings

SAUTÉED RAZOR CLAMS
with Hazelnut Lemon Sauce

Pazzo Ristorante, Portland, Oregon

Razor clams have a distinctive nutty sweetness that many people are passionate about. In this recipe, executive chef David Machado accents the nutty flavor of the clams with toasted hazelnuts, using fresh lemon and dry white wine as a contrast. This serves four as a dainty appetizer or one person as a main course.

¼ cup all-purpose flour	½ teaspoon freshly squeezed lemon juice
Salt and freshly ground black pepper	2 tablespoons toasted, chopped hazelnuts
4 razor clams, shucked and cleaned	1 tablespoon minced shallot
(about 5 ounces)	¼ cup unsalted butter, cut in pieces and chilled
2 tablespoons olive oil	1 tablespoon minced flat-leaf (Italian) parsley
½ cup pinot gris or other dry white wine	Flat-leaf (Italian) parsley sprigs, for garnish

MIX THE FLOUR with a pinch each of salt and pepper on a plate. Dredge the clams in the flour, patting to remove excess.

HEAT THE OIL in a medium skillet over medium-high heat. Add the clams and sauté until golden brown, about 30 seconds on each side; do not overcook. Transfer the clams to a plate and keep warm.

ADD THE WINE and lemon juice to the skillet, stirring to dissolve flavorful bits. Boil to reduce slightly, about 1 minute. Add the hazelnuts and shallot and cook for 30 seconds longer. Whisk in the cold butter until it has melted and the sauce has a rich consistency. Stir in the parsley, adding salt and pepper to taste.

ARRANGE THE CLAMS on a warm serving platter or individual plates, pour the sauce over them, and garnish with sprigs of parsley. Serve immediately.

Makes 4 servings

NORTHWEST RAZOR CLAMS

Named for their oblong shell that resembles an old-fashioned straight razor, Northwest razor clams (*Siliqua patula*) are found along sandy ocean beaches from California north to Alaska. Their sweet, succulent, creamy white meat is considered a delicacy by many seafood lovers. The key to good-tasting razor clams is freshness. The flesh should smell sweet like the sea and be creamy white. There is a significant change in the odor and color of clams that have been out of the water for more than three days. If the clams smell fishy, or if the flesh has darkened, don't buy them.

POLENTA-ENCRUSTED CRAB
with Wild Mushroom Tapenade

Bay Cafe, Lopez Island, Washington

Filled with sweet Dungeness crab, these savory polenta "muffins" are topped with a wild mushroom tapenade. Match this appetizer with a rich, dry riesling.

½ pound Dungeness crabmeat | *½ cup grated Parmesan cheese*
2 cups milk | *½ cup grated Swiss cheese*
2 cups water | *Salt and freshly ground black pepper*
1 cup polenta-grind (coarse) cornmeal |

MUSHROOM TAPENADE

2 tablespoons olive oil | *¼ cup minced flat-leaf (Italian) parsley*
6 ounces wild mushrooms (boletus, chanterelle, | *3 tablespoons chopped sun-dried tomatoes*
oyster, and/or shiitake mushrooms), | *(oil-packed)*
cleaned, trimmed, and sliced | *2 tablespoons capers*
2 cloves garlic, minced | *1 tablespoon freshly squeezed lemon juice*
½ cup chicken stock (see page 81) |

FOR THE TAPENADE, heat the olive oil in a medium-sized skillet, add the mushrooms and garlic, and sauté for 2 minutes over medium-high heat. Add the chicken stock, reduce the heat, and simmer until the mushrooms are very tender and most of the liquid has been absorbed, 15 to 20 minutes. Transfer the mixture to a bowl, add the parsley, sun-dried tomatoes, capers, and lemon juice, and toss to mix well. Set aside. The tapenade can be made a day in advance.

REMOVE ANY BITS of shell or cartilage from the crabmeat.

COMBINE THE MILK, water, and cornmeal in a medium-sized, heavy saucepan and bring to a boil, whisking constantly. Reduce the heat to medium and continue cooking for 20 minutes, whisking often. Remove the pan from the heat and stir in the Parmesan and Swiss cheeses, adding salt and pepper to taste.

LIGHTLY GREASE a 12-cup muffin tin. Half-fill each of the cups with the warm polenta mixture. Divide the crabmeat evenly among the muffin cups, pressing it gently into the polenta. Top the crab with the remaining polenta and use your fingers, moistened with water, to smooth the tops. Refrigerate until thoroughly chilled, at least 30 minutes. The polenta can be prepared to this point up to a day in advance.

PREHEAT THE OVEN to 350°F.

UNMOLD THE POLENTAS upside-down onto a lightly greased baking sheet and bake until very hot and lightly browned, 25 to 30 minutes. Set one polenta on each plate, top each with some of the mushroom tapenade, and serve.

Makes 12 servings

GARLIC CHEESECAKE

The Breadline Cafe, Omak, Washington

At the Breadline, this robust garlic cheesecake is served with a
drizzle of cilantro-lime pesto, sun-dried tomatoes, and Greek olives. For garlic
lovers, this dish is heaven. Take a little extra time and chop the garlic by hand;
pressing or processing the garlic releases more essential oils and makes the flavor
harsher. If you use pressed or processed garlic, use the lesser amount listed.
The intensity of the garlic can be cooled with a sparkling, citrusy
Hogue Cellars Columbia Valley Johannisberg riesling.

CRUST

1½ cups dry bread crumbs, | ¼ cup butter, melted
plain or seasoned | ¼ cup white wine

FILLING

16 ounces cream cheese, softened | 2 tablespoons whipping cream
3 eggs | 1 teaspoon lemon pepper
⅓ to ½ cup chopped garlic | or freshly ground black pepper
¼ cup all-purpose flour

TOPPING

1 cup sour cream | 1 tablespoon chopped garlic

PREHEAT THE OVEN to 325°F. Grease an 8- or 9-inch springform pan.

COMBINE THE BREAD CRUMBS, butter, and wine in a medium bowl. Pour the
crumb mixture into the prepared pan and pat the crumbs into an even crust along the
bottom and about 1½ inches up the sides. Set aside.

PUT THE CREAM CHEESE in the large bowl of an electric mixer. Beat in the eggs, one at a time, mixing thoroughly after each addition. Add the garlic, flour, cream, and lemon pepper. Continue mixing until well blended.

POUR THE CHEESECAKE filling into the prepared crust and bake until golden and firm, about 40 minutes. Meanwhile, combine the sour cream and garlic for the topping; set aside.

WHEN THE CHEESECAKE is done, remove it from the oven and let it sit for 5 minutes. Spread the sour cream mixture over the cake and let cool, then refrigerate for at least 2 hours. When the cheesecake is chilled and set, remove the rim of the spring-form pan, slice, and serve.

Makes 12 to 16 servings

NORTHWEST WINE

Each of the major wine regions in the Pacific Northwest, including wine-growing regions in Oregon, Washington, Idaho (on a small scale), and British Columbia, is renowned for producing outstanding and distinctive wines. Oregon is legendary for its elegant pinot noirs; delicate, food-friendly chardonnays; and spicy gewürztraminers and rieslings. Pinot gris, dubbed "the wine of the '90s" by some because of its affinity for lighter foods, is Oregon's rising star, with its luscious fruit and crisp acids.

Washington State, where most grapes are grown in desert conditions east of the Cascade Mountains, has received accolades for its robust, velvety merlots and cabernet sauvignons; its luscious, rich chardonnays; and its crisp, refreshing sauvignon blancs and semillons.

To the north, British Columbia's Okanagan Valley is setting trends with distinctive varietals, including spicy, floral *Ehrenfelser*; fruity *Maréchal Foch*; and lighter reds, including Chelois and Chancellor. British Columbia also produces fine examples of pinot noir, pinot gris, riesling, and sparkling wines.

MALAYSIAN CLAMS

Chef Bernard's Inn and Restaurant, Kimberley, British Columbia

The numerous dried chiles in this dish are very hot and aren't meant to be eaten; they are used only for seasoning. A serving of rice turns this appetizer into an entrée.

6 tablespoons olive oil	*2 tablespoons oyster sauce*
2 tablespoons minced red onion	*2 tablespoons chopped basil*
1 tablespoon minced garlic	*1 tablespoon Thai sweet black bean sauce*
2½ pounds Manila clams, scrubbed	*or other black bean sauce*
16 whole dried red chiles	*2 teaspoons Thai fish sauce (nam pla)*
1 cup sliced yellow onion	*or soy sauce*
(about ½ medium onion)	*2 teaspoons ground black pepper*
½ cup diced red bell pepper	*Basil sprigs, for garnish*
½ cup thinly sliced lemongrass	
(about 3 stalks)	

HEAT THE OLIVE OIL in a sauté pan or large, deep skillet. Add the red onion and garlic and cook over medium-high heat, stirring, until lightly browned, 1 to 2 minutes. Add the clams with the dried chiles and cook, stirring constantly, for 2 minutes. Add the sliced onion, bell pepper, lemongrass, oyster sauce, chopped basil, black bean sauce, fish sauce, and black pepper. Continue cooking, stirring constantly, until the clams have opened, 5 to 7 minutes longer. Discard any clams that do not open. Transfer the clams to a large platter or individual bowls, pour the sauce over them, and serve immediately, garnished with basil sprigs.

Makes 4 servings

PACIFIC NORTHWEST OYSTER WINES

"A loaf of bread," the Walrus said,
"Is what we chiefly need:
Pepper and vinegar besides
are very good indeed—
Now, if you're ready, Oysters dear,
we can begin to feed."
The Walrus and the Carpenter
by Lewis Carroll

The conniving, oyster-slurping Walrus in Lewis Carroll's "The Walrus and the Carpenter" certainly had his priorities straight when it came to eating oysters. Unfortunately, he and his wily colleague, the Carpenter, were negligent in assembling their picnic: They forgot the wine and, in doing so, missed one of the greatest gastronomic pleasures of all time.

Each year the Oregon Wine Advisory Board, the Washington Wine Commission, and the Pacific Coast Oyster Growers Association host the Pacific Northwest Oyster Wine Competition. With the help of oyster-loving wine experts, including chefs, restaurateurs, oyster growers, and wine and food writers, the ten best oyster wines are selected from more than one hundred submissions. Each wine is tasted blind with a freshly shucked Olympia oyster on the half shell.

Overall, the judges prefer dry white wines with crisp acids that slice right through the briny, metallic flavor of the oysters. Favorite varietals include chardonnay, pinot gris, chenin blanc, sauvignon blanc, semillon, and dry riesling.

When it comes to matchmaking oysters and wine, temperature is crucial, as is freshness. Make sure both wines and oysters are ice cold. Bury oysters in ice for about an hour before shucking, and chill wines thoroughly in a refrigerator or freezer. A fresh loaf of crusty sourdough or rye bread is essential. Butter is optional. Shuck the oysters just before serving, and arrange them on a bed of crushed ice.

GAZPACHO

Dykstra House Restaurant, Grandview, Washington

Made with garden-fresh vegetables from Eastern Washington, this chilled soup is a summertime favorite at the Dykstra House. When they're in season, Walla Walla Sweet onions are preferred. The chef recommends making the soup one day ahead so that the flavors can marry. If you will be serving the soup right away, you may want to add more V-8 juice; the vegetables will give off liquid as they sit. Spice this up with minced chiles or use spicy V-8 juice, if you like.

2 pounds vine-ripened tomatoes, finely diced
2 cucumbers, peeled and finely diced
2 cups V-8 juice
½ onion, preferably Walla Walla Sweet, finely diced
1 green bell pepper, cored, seeded, and finely diced

1 cup loosely packed cilantro leaves
2 tablespoons olive oil
2 tablespoons vinegar
2 large cloves garlic, minced
1 tablespoon freshly squeezed lemon juice
Salt and freshly ground black pepper

COMBINE THE TOMATOES, cucumbers, V-8 juice, onion, green pepper, cilantro, olive oil, vinegar, garlic, and lemon juice in a large, nonreactive bowl. Season to taste with salt and pepper, cover, and chill until ready to serve, preferably at least 4 hours.

Makes 6 to 8 servings

PALOUSE RED LENTIL–MINT SOUP

Cafe Langley, Langley, Washington

The Palouse region of Eastern Washington, with its gently
rolling hills, is renowned for red, green, and yellow lentils, which are
marketed worldwide. A member of the legume family, lentils are a good source
of vegetable protein. Cooked, they have a mild, nutty flavor, which is accented
in this recipe by mint. Look for lentils in the bulk food section of your
local supermarket; any color will work if red ones are not available.

¼ cup unsalted butter	¼ cup dried mint or
¾ cup chopped onion	½ cup minced fresh mint
1 tablespoon tomato paste	¼ teaspoon dried red pepper flakes
7 cups chicken stock (see page 81)	Salt
1 cup red lentils	Croutons, for garnish (optional)
2 tablespoons all-purpose flour	

HEAT 2 TABLESPOONS of the butter in a large pot, add the onion, and sauté over
medium heat until tender, 3 to 5 minutes. Stir in the tomato paste. Add the chicken
stock and lentils, cover, and simmer until the lentils are tender, about 20 minutes. Remove from the heat and let cool for a few minutes. Working in batches, purée the mixture in a food processor or blender until just smooth. Set aside in a large bowl.

MELT THE REMAINING 2 tablespoons butter in the same pot over medium heat,
add the flour, and whisk until the flour begins to turn golden, about 2 minutes. Gradually whisk in the lentil mixture and bring to a gentle simmer. Stir in the mint and red
pepper flakes, with salt to taste, and simmer 1 to 2 minutes longer. Ladle the soup into
individual bowls, garnish with croutons, if you like, and serve immediately.

Makes 4 to 6 servings

BASIC CHICKEN STOCK

Use whole chicken or meaty chicken parts for making stock,
then take advantage of the cooked meat for making chicken salad,
pasta dishes, or other favorite recipes that use cooked chicken meat.

*2 to 3 pounds chicken backs, necks,
or other portions, well rinsed
2 onions, quartered
2 large carrots, coarsely chopped
2 stalks celery, coarsely chopped*

*Bouquet garni of 3 parsley stems, 2
sprigs thyme, and 1 bay leaf, tied
together with string
1 teaspoon black peppercorns
12 cups water (more if needed)*

PUT THE CHICKEN parts in a stockpot with the onions, carrots,
celery, bouquet garni, and peppercorns. Add water to cover, and bring
just to a boil. Reduce the heat and simmer, uncovered, until the stock
is well flavored, about 2 hours. (If you are planning to use the meat
from the chicken, simmer the stock only 45 to 50 minutes and let the
chicken cool in the stock.) If necessary, add more hot water to the pot
as it simmers so that the bones are always covered. Use a large spoon
to skim off scum that rises to the top.

STRAIN THE STOCK through a fine sieve or a colander lined with
cheesecloth, discarding the solids. Let cool, then skim off fat that rises to
the surface. Chill and use within a few days, or freeze for up to 1 month.

Makes about 8 cups

MARS'S OYSTER STEW

Maple Leaf Grill, Seattle, Washington

Rich, thick, and creamy, this untraditional oyster stew from chef Rip Ripley is flavored with Cajun-spiced, cured tasso ham and artichoke hearts. Ripley got the idea for this stew from his friend Margaret "Mars" Clark and named it after her. If you can't find tasso ham, substitute another ham and add a pinch of Cajun seasoning to the stew. You can shuck the oysters yourself, or use the excellent-quality oysters that are sold in jars in many areas. Look for ones labeled "extra small." When oysters aren't in season, chef Rip suggests using rock shrimp as a substitute.

2 tablespoons olive oil	3 cups whipping cream
1 medium onion, diced	2 dozen extra-small oysters, shucked
6 ounces tasso ham, cut in julienne strips	1 can (13 ounces) artichoke hearts,
2 teaspoons dried oregano	drained and quartered
2 cups chicken stock (see page 81)	1 cup spinach (about 1 ounce), cut in
or fish stock (see page 83)	thin strips
1 cup white wine	3 to 4 cups steamed white rice

HEAT THE OLIVE OIL in a medium saucepan, add the onion, and sauté over medium-high heat until softened but not browned, 3 to 5 minutes. Add the ham and oregano and sauté for 1 minute longer. Add the stock and wine, bring to a boil, and boil until reduced by about two-thirds (down to about 1 cup), 10 to 12 minutes. Add the cream and return to a boil. Add the oysters and artichoke hearts, reduce the heat, and simmer until the oysters plump and the edges begin to curl, about 3 minutes.

DIVIDE THE SPINACH among 4 individual bowls, and ladle the oyster stew over it. Serve the steamed rice on the side.

Makes 4 servings

BASIC FISH STOCK

Fish stock takes only 20 minutes to make. White fish bones are best for making stock, halibut bones being among the best. Stock can also be made from shrimp shells peeled from raw shrimp. In many recipes, clam nectar diluted with water can be used in place of fish stock.

2 pounds fish bones, cut in pieces,	*Bouquet garni of 3 sprigs of parsley*
and/or fish heads	*2 sprigs thyme, and 1 bay leaf,*
1 onion, sliced	*tied together with string*
1 large carrot, sliced	*½ teaspoon black peppercorns*
2 stalks celery, sliced	*6 cups water, more if needed*

WASH THE FISH bones and heads thoroughly in cold water; remove and discard gills if they are still present.

COMBINE THE FISH bones, onion, carrot, celery, bouquet garni, and peppercorns in a stockpot. Add the water; it should completely cover the other ingredients. Bring slowly to a boil, and simmer, uncovered, for 20 minutes. Use a large spoon to skim off scum that rises to the top.

STRAIN THE STOCK through a fine sieve or a colander lined with cheesecloth, discarding the solids. Chill and use within a few days, or freeze for up to 1 month.

Makes about 4 cups

WILD MUSHROOM AND SHERRY BISQUE

Stephanie Inn, Cannon Beach, Oregon

At the Stephanie Inn, executive chef Rob Schulz garnishes this soup with parsley oil (made by puréeing 1 bunch of Italian parsley in a blender with ½ cup olive oil) and port syrup (made by reducing 1 bottle of port over medium heat until thickened). The two sauces are dispensed from squeeze bottles. You may want to simply stir in a little more sherry just before serving.

½ cup butter	*1 teaspoon minced rosemary*
½ cup all-purpose flour	*1 cup dry sherry*
1½ pounds mixed wild mushrooms	*2½ cups vegetable stock or*
(chanterelles, boletus, oyster, matsutake),	*chicken stock (see page 81)*
cleaned and trimmed	*2½ cups whipping cream*
3 tablespoons olive oil	*Salt and freshly ground white or black pepper*
1 medium onion, diced	*2 teaspoons minced oregano*
5 cloves garlic, minced	

PREPARE A ROUX by melting the butter in a small, heavy pan, stirring in the flour, and cooking over medium heat, stirring often, until the mixture forms a thick paste and has a slight toasty aroma, 4 to 5 minutes. The roux should not brown. Set aside to cool.

SLICE THE MUSHROOMS and set aside about 2 cups of mixed mushrooms for garnish.

HEAT 2 TABLESPOONS of the olive oil in a large, heavy pot until very hot. Add the mushrooms, onion, half the garlic, and the rosemary. Sauté over medium-high heat until the mushrooms are tender and the onions are lightly browned and caramelized, about 10 minutes. Add the sherry, bring to a boil, and boil to reduce the liquid by half. Add the stock and cream, return to a boil, then reduce the heat to keep the mixture at a simmer. Stir in the roux, a couple of tablespoons at a time, mixing well after each addition, until the soup is thick enough to coat the back of a spoon; you may not need all of the roux.

PASS THE SOUP through a food mill and return it to the soup pot. Alternatively, process the soup in batches in a food processor or blender; the soup should be fairly smooth but still have some texture. Season to taste with salt and pepper. Keep the soup warm over very low heat.

HEAT THE REMAINING tablespoon of oil in a medium skillet and add the reserved mushrooms with the remaining garlic and the oregano. Sauté over medium-high heat until the mushrooms are just tender and the garlic is fragrant, 3 to 4 minutes.

LADLE THE BISQUE into individual bowls and garnish each with some of the sautéed mushrooms. Serve immediately.

Makes 6 servings

LOPEZ ISLAND MUSSEL SOUP
with Saffron and Cream

Friday Harbor House, San Juan Island, Washington

"My menu planning is governed by the season," says chef Greg Atkinson, who features local mussels from Shoal Bay Shellfish Farm on Lopez Island in this creamy soup. "These mussels are delivered only during cooler months, when the mollusks are at their best," he explains. During summer months look for Mediterranean mussels, which are at their prime then.

2 cups off-dry white wine, such as	2 cups whipping cream
Lopez Island Madeleine Angevine	Generous pinch of saffron threads, preferably
1 tablespoon chopped garlic	Spanish, steeped in 2 tablespoons warm
3 pounds mussels, cleaned and debearded	water for 15 minutes
2 tablespoons butter	6 leaves spinach or sorrel, cut into fine
2 tablespoons all-purpose flour	ribbons, for garnish

COMBINE THE WINE and garlic in a kettle over high heat and bring to a boil. Add the mussels, cover, and steam until they begin to open, about 3 minutes. Transfer opened mussels to a bowl, using a slotted spoon. Continue steaming until all have opened, 2 to 3 minutes longer. Discard any mussels that do not open. Reserve the cooking liquid. As soon as the mussels are cool enough to handle, remove them from their shells and put them in the cooking liquid.

MELT THE BUTTER in a large saucepan. Whisk in the flour and cook, stirring, for 1 minute. Add the cream and bring to a boil, whisking constantly. Add the saffron and its steeping liquid along with the mussels and their cooking liquid. Bring the soup to a gentle boil, and serve hot, garnishing each bowl with fine ribbons of spinach or sorrel.

Makes 6 servings

MUSSEL MANIA

Mussels have been relished in Europe for centuries. Thanks to the emergence of a handful of quality mussel farms throughout the Northwest and to the recent introduction of the winter-spawning Mediterranean mussel, they are finally catching on here.

Mussels are bivalves. Some mussels burrow in soft wood or clay, but the majority anchor themselves to rocks, pilings, or other underwater objects by a byssus, or "beard." Four species of mussels are commonly used in Northwest cookery: the Puget Sound blue mussel, the wild Pacific Ocean mussel, the Mediterranean mussel, and the East Coast blue mussel.

Native to protected waters of northern Puget Sound, British Columbia, and Alaska is the Puget Sound blue mussel (also called black or bay mussel). Similar in look and flavor to the Mediterranean mussel, but smaller, this is the mussel raised by Penn Cove Mussels of Whidbey Island, the oldest commercial mussel farm in North America.

The wild Pacific Ocean mussel is a blue-black mussel found throughout the coastal waters of the Northwest. These mussels are hardier, with a wilder, stronger flavor.

The Mediterranean mussel was recently discovered growing in protected bays in California and Oregon. This is the famous blue mussel of Spain, the world leader in farmed mussel production. No one is sure how these mussels found their way to the Northwest, but judging by the size of established colonies, experts speculate that they have lived here for many years, probably arriving as stowaways adhered to the bottoms of Spanish galleons. The smooth shell of these black-blue mussels has a shimmering blue interior, and the meat is sweet and succulent. Mediterranean mussels are winter spawners, meaning they are at their prime in the heat of summer.

The East Coast blue mussel, sometimes available in Northwest markets, is currently farmed in Canada. The green-lipped mussel from New Zealand is also appearing in markets here.

MUSSELS IN CORN CHOWDER

The Inn at Langley, Langley, Washington

Summertime, when corn is at its peak, is the best time to make this delicious chowder, created by innkeeper/chef Stephen Nogal for his guests at The Inn at Langley. If fresh corn is unavailable, frozen is a decent substitute. You'll want to round out the meal with lots of crusty bread, and Nogal recommends a Chinook sauvingnon blanc or L'Ecole semillon as an ideal accompaniment.

3 cups chicken stock (see page 81)
or fish stock (see page 83)
1 cup dry white wine
¼ cup butter
½ cup all-purpose flour
1 pound freshly cut or frozen corn kernels
(thaw if frozen) (about 4 cups)

1½ cups whipping cream
Sea salt and freshly ground black pepper
2 tablespoons peanut oil
2 pounds mussels, cleaned and debearded
1 or 2 red bell peppers, cored, seeded,
and diced
1 bunch flat-leaf (Italian) parsley, chopped

BRING THE STOCK and wine to a boil in a medium saucepan, reduce the heat to low, and simmer gently. In a large, heavy pot, melt the butter over medium heat, add the flour, and whisk until the flour begins to turn golden, about 2 minutes. Whisk in about 1 cup of the hot stock and continue whisking until the mixture is very thick. Add the remaining stock, return to a boil, and simmer gently until thickened, 8 to 10 minutes. Add half of the corn and simmer 5 minutes longer. Remove from the heat.

PRESS THE MIXTURE through a food mill or sieve in batches. Do not purée in a food processor. Return the corn mixture to the pot, stir in the cream, and season to taste with salt and pepper. Keep hot.

HEAT THE PEANUT OIL in a wok or large skillet over medium-high heat. When the oil just begins to smoke, add the mussels and the red peppers, stirring to coat them evenly in oil. Cover the wok and cook until the first few mussels open, about 3 minutes. Pour the hot corn chowder over the mussels, stir to mix, cover, and continue cooking until all the mussels have opened, 2 to 3 minutes longer. Discard any mussels that do not open. Stir in the remaining corn and taste the soup for seasoning. Ladle the mussel chowder mixture into warmed soup bowls, sprinkle with chopped parsley, and serve.

Makes 4 servings

STORING AND CLEANING LIVE MUSSELS

Place the mussels in an open container, cover with a moist cloth, and refrigerate for up to three days. Before cooking, discard any that are not alive (the shells should be tightly closed, or should close when tapped). Also, check for "mudders" by trying to slide the two halves of the shell across each other. If they budge, the shells may be filled with mud.

Before cooking the mussels, scrub them with a stiff brush under cold water. If desired, remove the byssus, or beard, by pulling it from the mussel with the back of a small knife or with your fingers. Pull toward the wide end of the shell. This should be done just before cooking because mussels die once they are debearded. You can also debeard mussels after they are steamed.

ROASTED-GARLIC PUMPKIN BISQUE
with Herb Potato Dumplings

Inn at Ludlow Bay, Port Ludlow, Washington

Topped with lightly herbed potato dumplings, this is a rich, hearty
soup that captures the flavors of a Northwest fall. Not all pumpkins are good
for eating; many are raised for sturdy jack-o'-lantern purposes. Ask your produce
manager for a cooking variety. Any sweet, firm, meaty yellow squash, such
as Hubbard or acorn squash, makes a good substitute.

1 whole head garlic	*½ cup whipping cream*
2½ pounds fresh pumpkin,	*1 to 2 tablespoons packed brown sugar*
peeled and seeded	*¼ teaspoon ground nutmeg*
4 cups chicken stock (see page 81)	*Salt and freshly ground black pepper*
1 small onion, diced	*Crème fraîche or sour cream, for serving*

HERB POTATO DUMPLINGS

2 medium russet potatoes	*¼ cup chopped mixed herbs, such as flat-leaf*
(about 1½ pounds)	*(Italian) parsley, chives, thyme, and oregano*
2 egg yolks	*½ cup all-purpose flour (more if needed)*

PREHEAT THE OVEN to 400°F.

DISCARD THE LOOSE, PAPERY outer skin from the garlic head and wrap it in a
piece of foil. Roast the garlic in the oven until tender, about 30 minutes. At the same
time, bake the potatoes for the dumplings until tender, about 50 minutes.

WHILE THE GARLIC and potatoes are baking, cut the pumpkin into large chunks and
put it in a large pot with the chicken stock and onion. Bring to a boil and simmer until
the pumpkin is tender, 20 to 30 minutes.

UNWRAP THE GARLIC and let cool slightly, then peel the individual cloves. Lightly mash the garlic with a fork in a small bowl (you should have about 2 tablespoons); set aside.

WORKING IN BATCHES, purée the pumpkin mixture in a food processor or blender and return it to the pot. Stir in the cream, roasted garlic, brown sugar, and nutmeg, with salt and pepper to taste. Keep warm over very low heat while making the dumplings.

BRING A LARGE pot of lightly salted water to a boil.

HALVE THE BAKED POTATOES and peel away all the brown skin. Mash the potatoes. Stir in the egg yolks and herbs, along with a pinch each of salt and pepper. Stir in the flour, a little at a time, until a firm dough is formed.

PUT THE DOUGH on a lightly floured work surface and roll it into a cylinder about ¾ inch in diameter. Cut the cylinder into 1-inch slices to form the dumplings. Cook the dumplings in batches in the boiling water until they are tender and float to the surface, about 2 to 4 minutes. Scoop out with a slotted spoon and drain well.

TO SERVE, ladle the hot pumpkin bisque into individual bowls and add the potato dumplings to the center of each bowl. Drizzle crème fraîche over the soup and serve.

Makes 4 to 6 servings

CREAMY ONION SOUP
with Bay Shrimp

Bay House, Lincoln City, Oregon

Located on the banks of Siletz Bay, the Bay House has access
to plenty of fresh seafood, including sweet, locally harvested Oregon bay shrimp.
Whenever Walla Walla Sweet onions are in season, chef Greg Meixner combines
the two summer specialties in this creamy, rich soup. To caramelize the onions,
which gives a distinctive flavor to this soup, you may need to cook them longer or
drain off some of the liquid. Adding butter (as suggested) and a teaspoon
or two of sugar also helps the caramelizing process.

¼ cup olive oil	3 tablespoons uncooked basmati rice
½ cup butter (optional, for caramelizing)	1 teaspoon dried thyme
4 pounds sweet onions, preferably Walla Walla	Salt and freshly ground black pepper
Sweets, diced	2 cups whipping cream
2 cups bottled clam juice	½ to ¾ pound cooked bay shrimp
¼ cup dry white wine	Fresh thyme leaves, for garnish
¼ cup marsala	

HEAT THE OIL and butter, if using, in a large pot over medium-high heat. Add the
onions and sauté until well browned and caramelized, about 30 minutes, stirring frequently. Stir in the clam juice, wine, marsala, rice, and thyme with a good pinch each
of salt and pepper. Bring to a boil, then reduce the heat and simmer, stirring occasionally,
until the rice is very tender, about 30 minutes.

WORKING IN BATCHES, purée the soup in a food processor or blender until
smooth. Return the soup to the pot and stir in the cream. Reheat the soup until very
hot; taste for seasoning.

DIVIDE THE SHRIMP evenly among individual bowls. Ladle the hot soup over the
shrimp and garnish each bowl with a sprinkle of thyme leaves. Serve immediately.

Makes 6 servings

CORN AND CHEESE CHOWDER

Grateful Bread Bakery & Restaurant, Pacific City, Oregon

Lightly spiced with cumin and spiked with sharp Tillamook cheddar cheese, this hearty soup is best when made with freshly harvested corn. Served with robust breads or muffins, it makes a satisfying lunch or light supper.

1½ pounds potatoes, peeled and	*¼ cup all-purpose flour*
cut in 1-inch dice (about 4 cups)	*2½ cups half-and-half*
4 cups water	*2 cups corn kernels*
1 teaspoon cumin seed	*8 to 10 ounces sharp cheddar cheese,*
½ cup butter	*preferably Tillamook, grated*
2 large onions, chopped	

COMBINE THE POTATOES, water, and cumin in a large pot and bring to a boil. Lower the heat and simmer until the potatoes are just tender, about 15 minutes. Do not drain the potatoes.

WHILE THE POTATOES are cooking, heat the butter in a large skillet, add the onions, and cook, stirring occasionally, over medium heat until tender, about 8 to 10 minutes. Sprinkle the flour over the onions and continue cooking for a few minutes, stirring to mix well.

ADD THE ONION MIXTURE to the potatoes and their cooking water, then add the half-and-half, corn, and salt and pepper to taste. Simmer the soup until thickened, about 20 minutes, stirring occasionally.

SPRINKLE ABOUT HALF of the cheese in the bottom of individual soup bowls. Ladle the chowder over and sprinkle the remaining cheese on top. Serve immediately. Diners should stir the cheese into the soup before eating.

Makes 6 to 8 servings

FISHERMAN'S STEW

La Serre Restaurant, Yachats, Oregon

Featuring the catch of the day from the seaside fishing village of
Yachats, on the Oregon coast, this flavorful, tomato-based stew is brimming
with Dungeness crab, freshly shucked oysters, shrimp, clams, and mussels. Serve
with sourdough bread and a glass of bright, fruity pinot noir, such as
Rex Hill's Kings Ridge pinot noir from Oregon.

2 to 3 tablespoons olive oil	*1 teaspoon minced basil, or ½ teaspoon dried*
1 onion, minced	*1 teaspoon salt*
1 stalk celery, minced	*½ teaspoon freshly ground black pepper*
½ green bell pepper,	*1½ pounds steamer clams, scrubbed*
cored, seeded, and minced	*¾ pound lingcod, skin and pin bones*
1 clove garlic, crushed	*removed, cut into serving pieces*
4 cups chopped ripe tomatoes (about 2	*1½ pounds mussels, cleaned*
pounds) or 1 can (28 ounces)	*and debearded*
chopped tomatoes, drained	*12 large shrimp, peeled and deveined*
1½ cups water	*1 cooked Dungeness crab, cleaned and cracked*
1 cup dry red wine	*into serving pieces*
¼ cup tomato paste	*12 oysters, shucked*
1 bay leaf, crumbled	*6 ounces cooked bay shrimp*
1 teaspoon minced oregano,	*2 tablespoons minced flat-leaf (Italian) parsley,*
or ½ teaspoon dried	*for garnish*

HEAT THE OIL in a large pot, add the onion, celery, green pepper, and garlic, and sauté
over medium heat until tender and lightly browned, about 5 minutes. Add the tomatoes,
water, red wine, tomato paste, bay leaf, oregano, basil, salt, and pepper. Bring just to a
boil, lower the heat, cover the pot, and simmer until the sauce is thick, about 1½ hours.

ADD THE CLAMS to the pot, followed by the lingcod, mussels, and raw shrimp. Cover and cook over medium heat for 5 minutes. Gently stir in the crab pieces, oysters, and bay shrimp, and continue simmering until the clams and mussels have opened and the remaining seafood is cooked through, about 10 minutes longer. (If some of the seafood is cooked before the rest, remove it and set aside, covered, to keep warm.)

DIVIDE THE SEAFOOD evenly among individual bowls and pour the sauce over it. Sprinkle each serving with parsley and serve.

Makes 6 servings

DUNGENESS CRAB

Many seafood lovers consider sweet, buttery-rich Dungeness crab to be the best eating crab in the world. "Dungeness crab," said James Beard, "is sheer unadulterated crab heaven."

The range of this succulent crustacean extends from Monterey Bay in California north to Alaska. Dungeness crab is available most of the year. The largest Dungeness crabs are taken from Alaskan waters, where the minimum catch standard is 6¼ inches across the shell. Only male crabs may be harvested.

Dungeness crabs are sold live, cooked, or cooked and frozen. Whenever possible, buy live rather than precooked crab; your chances of getting a better-quality product are much greater because commercial crab cookers cook all crabs for the same amount of time, regardless of their weight, overcooking all but the largest crabs.

Live crabs should be purchased within one week of harvest, and cooked the same day you buy them. Chill them thoroughly before cooking by packing them in ice and covering them with a damp towel. (If crabs are warm when you drop them into boiling water, they are more likely to drop a leg or two.) Chilled crabs become sluggish, but they should still move their legs and mouths when provoked.

DUNGENESS CRAB
with Ocean Salad

Rover's, Seattle, Washington

This crab salad from chef Thierry Rautureau resounds with the flavors
of the briny sea. It is made with ocean salad (a toss of fresh edible seaweeds
marinated in sesame oil, chiles, mirin, and soy sauce) which is available, premixed,
at some Northwest grocery stores and seafood markets. Or try fresh steamed
asparagus, or a salad of mixed greens, tossed with vinaigrette, as a side.

2 cups (about ¾ pound)	*½ yellow bell pepper, cored, seeded,*
Dungeness crabmeat	*and finely diced*
7 ounces ocean salad	*¼ pound snow peas, blanched, drained,*
½ red bell pepper, cored, seeded,	*and thinly sliced*
and finely diced	*1 tablespoon minced shallot*

HORSERADISH AIOLI

2 egg yolks	*½ cup extra-virgin olive oil*
2 cloves garlic, minced	*1 tablespoon minced chives*
1½ teaspoons Dijon-style mustard	*1 tablespoon vinegar*
1½ teaspoons prepared horseradish	*Salt and freshly ground black pepper*

FOR THE AIOLI, combine the egg yolks, garlic, mustard, and horseradish in a food
processor. With the machine running, add the oil, drizzling it very slowly at first. Once
the mixture begins to emulsify, continue adding the oil in a steady stream. Add the
chives, vinegar, and salt and pepper to taste. Set aside.

REMOVE ANY BITS of shell or cartilage from the crabmeat. Coarsely chop enough of the ocean salad to make 3 tablespoons; set the rest aside.

COMBINE THE CRABMEAT, chopped ocean salad, bell peppers, snow peas, and shallot in a large bowl. Toss to mix well, and season to taste with salt and pepper.

ARRANGE THE CRAB SALAD in mounds on individual plates, placing the remaining ocean salad alongside it. Drizzle with the horseradish aioli and serve.

Makes 6 to 8 servings

BUYING DUNGENESS CRAB

When buying Dungeness crab, be selective. Use your senses to find the freshest ones available.

Look: The legs and shell should all be intact. The crab's shell should be clean, brightly colored, and free from cracks or punctures. Live crabs should be violet and beige. Cooked crabs should be bright red.

Touch: The crab should feel heavy for its size (this means that the meat fills the shell). The shell should feel hard (soft shells mean that the crab has not finished molting). Feel the back of cooked crabs to make sure they are very cold; otherwise unwanted bacteria may have started to grow.

Listen: Tap the shell; the crab should sound firm and solid, not hollow.

Smell: Fresh or cooked crabs should smell sweet and clean, like the ocean. Older crabs will smell like sweaty tennis shoes or, worse, ammonia.

Taste: If the crab is precooked, ask to sample a leg. The meat should taste sweet and clean and should not be too salty.

COOKING DUNGENESS CRAB

Cook crabs in boiling sea water or salt water (½ pound of kosher salt per gallon of water gives the same salinity as sea water) for 8 to 10 minutes per pound. Once the crabs are cooked, transfer them immediately to a sink or bowl filled with ice water, and chill thoroughly before serving. Eat fresh crab within three days of cooking.

To clean the cooked crab, first pry off the top shell. Then remove the V-shaped abdominal shield or "apron" from the underside of the crab. Holding the crab under cold running water, use your thumbs to scrape away the gills and liver from the sides of the crab cavity.

Anyone who's been frustrated trying to crack crab using a nutcracker will be happy to learn there's a much more efficient way—with a mallet. Using your hands, break the crab body into two halves. Remove the legs and claws from the body. Crack the body sections by placing them on a firm surface and crushing them under the palm of your hand. Using a wooden or metal mallet, crack each claw section by placing the claw, edge side up, over the center of a double sink or on a board and striking firmly with the mallet to split the shell (do not strike so hard that you crush the meat). Crack each leg gently, holding them on edge.

When serving Dungeness crab, allow ½ to 1 whole crab per person. Clean and precrack crabs and serve with melted butter or with your favorite sauce.

Cover the table with butcher paper or layers of newspaper and have plenty of napkins on hand. Finger bowls filled with hot tea and lemon slices will clean sticky fingers admirably (the tannin from the tea and acid from the lemon cut right through the fat in the crab). And have hot towels available for wiping hands. Once the table is set, tie on a bib, roll up your sleeves, and dive in.

NORTHWEST CAESAR SALAD

Colophon Cafe, Bellingham, Washington

Lighter and easier to prepare than the classic Caesar salad, this
variation is made without the raw egg used in most Caesar dressings. You could
substitute sautéed squid or scallops for the shrimp or smoked salmon.

½ cup olive oil	*1 small head romaine lettuce, rinsed and*
3 or 4 cloves garlic, minced	*dried*
1 tablespoon freshly squeezed	*1 small head green-leaf lettuce,*
lemon juice, or to taste	*rinsed and dried*
2 teaspoons Worcestershire sauce	*¼ cup grated Parmesan cheese*
1 teaspoon Dijon-style mustard	*1 cup cooked shrimp or flaked smoked*
Salt and freshly ground black pepper	*salmon (about 6 ounces)*

COLOPHON CROUTONS

4 cups cubed day-old bread	*1 teaspoon thyme leaves*
½ cup butter, melted	*1 teaspoon minced flat-leaf (Italian) parsley*
1 clove garlic, minced	*1 teaspoon minced tarragon*

FOR THE CROUTONS, preheat the oven to 325°F. Scatter the bread cubes in an even
layer on a baking sheet. In a small bowl, combine the butter, garlic, thyme, parsley, and
tarragon. Drizzle the butter mixture over the bread cubes and stir to evenly coat the
bread. Bake for about 18 minutes, stirring once after 8 minutes, until nicely browned
and crunchy. Set aside to cool.

COMBINE THE OLIVE OIL, garlic, lemon juice, Worcestershire sauce, mustard, and salt
and pepper to taste in a jar with a tight-fitting lid and shake well to mix.

TEAR THE ROMAINE and green-leaf lettuce into large pieces and put them in a large
bowl. Add the Parmesan cheese, shrimp, and cooled croutons and toss. Shake the dressing
to mix, drizzle it over the salad, and toss to coat well. Serve immediately.

Makes 2 to 4 servings

DUFFY'S DAWN SALAD

The Breadline Cafe, Omak, Washington

Duffy Bishop, queen of Northwest rhythm and blues and an occasional performer at the Breadline Cafe, is the inspiration behind this full-meal salad. For the apple garnish, the Breadline sometimes substitutes a local pear poached in merlot wine. When you buy the smoked turkey, make sure it's in a chunk, rather than thinly sliced, so you can cut it into cubes.

1 pound smoked turkey, cut into ½-inch cubes	2 tablespoons toasted sliced almonds
4 ounces provolone cheese, cut into ¼-inch cubes	2 tablespoons dried cranberries
1 large head romaine, rinsed and torn into salad-sized pieces	Sliced Granny Smith apple, for garnish

OKANOGAN APPLE DRESSING

¾ cup grated tart apple, with peel (about 1 medium apple)	1 tablespoon apple cider vinegar
¾ cup apple cider	¾ teaspoon minced garlic
½ cup vegetable oil	¼ teaspoon ground cinnamon
2 tablespoons freshly squeezed lemon juice	¼ teaspoon ground cardamom

FOR THE DRESSING, combine the apple, cider, oil, lemon juice, vinegar, garlic, cinnamon, and cardamom in a medium bowl and stir to mix. Set aside.

COMBINE THE SMOKED TURKEY, provolone, and romaine in a large bowl. Pour the apple dressing over the salad and toss to mix. Arrange the salad on individual plates, sprinkle with the toasted almonds and dried cranberries, and garnish with slices of apple. Serve immediately.

Makes 4 servings

AN APPLE A DAY

If you followed the age-old advice and ate an apple a day, sampling a new variety each day, it would take at least twenty-seven years to taste the 10,000 or more varieties of apples that exist. Chances are you would never run out of apples.

"Apples are like roses," says apple grower Alan Foster of Newberg, Oregon. "There is unlimited potential for breeding apples, so we'll never run out of new varieties."

Washington State leads the country in apple production, producing some 2.4 million tons of apples each year. Stacked one by one, this quantity of apples would stretch to the moon and halfway back.

Although more than 20 apple varieties are grown commercially in Washington, two of every three apples grown in the state are Red Delicious. To please consumers, growers continued breeding redder and redder Red Delicious apples. "Unfortunately, in our zeal for producing the most beautiful apple, we forgot about the most important part—taste!" says apple grower Dick Olsen, who, with his brother Larry, owns 18,000 acres of farmland in Prosser, Washington.

Although Olsen believes that Red Delicious will remain king of the apples for the next ten or more years, he and his brother are also looking toward the future by growing and marketing different varieties. They have planted half of their orchards in so-called new or exotic apples—Fuji, Gala, Elstar, Braeburn, and Criterion. "Fujis are so spectacular, they are bound to replace some older varieties," says Larry Olsen. "They are great for eating or cooking, store extremely well, and will win converts easily on their quality alone."

The Olsens recommend storing apples in the refrigerator. Other growers suggest wrapping apples individually in newspaper and storing them in a cool place at uniform temperature, either in the refrigerator or in an unheated basement.

ENDIVE AND HOOD RIVER APPLES
with Spiced Pecans, Goat Cheese,
and Sherry Vinaigrette

RiverPlace Hotel, Portland, Oregon

Noted for its slightly bitter, nutty flavor, Belgian endive (or witloof chicory) is a small, cone-shaped salad green with slender 5- to 6-inch leaves that are tightly packed. Look for creamy white leaves with pale yellow tips and no blemishes. The chef at River Place suggests experimenting with different goat cheeses, as they all have different characters. Also, he recommends seeking out the oldest sherry vinegar you can find, as these vinegars mellow with age.

6 heads Belgian endive (about 1½ pounds)
2 red apples, preferably Gala or Fuji, cored and cut in thin strips

6 ounces goat cheese, crumbled
Crushed pink peppercorns, for garnish
Minced chives, for garnish

SPICED PECANS

1 tablespoon butter
1 tablespoon honey
½ teaspoon ground coriander
½ teaspoon ground fennel seed
½ teaspoon ground cardamom
¼ teaspoon ground cinnamon

¼ teaspoon ground mace
¼ teaspoon salt
⅛ teaspoon ground cayenne
⅛ teaspoon ground cloves
4 ounces pecan pieces

SHERRY VINAIGRETTE

¼ cup walnut oil
¼ cup vegetable oil
2 tablespoons aged sherry vinegar

2 tablespoons freshly squeezed orange juice
Salt and freshly ground white or black pepper

FOR THE PECANS, preheat the oven to 350°F. Melt the butter with the honey in a small saucepan and stir in the spices. Add the pecan pieces and stir until thoroughly coated in the spice mixture. Spread the pecans evenly onto a nonstick or lightly greased baking sheet. Bake until the nuts are crisp, 12 to 15 minutes. Set aside to cool.

FOR THE VINAIGRETTE, combine the walnut oil, vegetable oil, vinegar, and orange juice in a small bowl. Whisk to mix well, then add salt and pepper to taste. Set aside.

TRIM THE CORES from the endive and remove three large, outer leaves from each head. Arrange three of the leaves, like the spokes of a wheel, on each of 6 plates. Cut the remaining endive into julienne strips and put it in a large bowl with the apples, goat cheese, and spiced pecans.

WHISK THE VINAIGRETTE to mix, then pour about ⅓ cup of it over the endive mixture. Toss to mix well so that some of the goat cheese blends with the vinaigrette to thicken it slightly (the chef suggests using your hands to toss the salad). Taste the salad for seasoning, adding more dressing to taste. Pile some of the salad in the center of each plate. Sprinkle the crushed peppercorns and chives over the salad and serve.

Makes 6 servings

BEYOND THE BIG THREE

Red Delicious, Golden Delicious, and Granny Smith are the big sellers in the Northwest, but our markets offer many less-familiar varieties. Here are just a few you might like to try.

Fuji: Developed in Japan in the 1930s, Fuji is a cross between Red Delicious and Ralls Janet. It is red with a green to yellow background. The flesh is firm, crisp, and juicy, with sweet apple and pear notes. Fuji retains its shape well during cooking and is also good eaten fresh or in salads.

Gala: Developed in New Zealand in 1939 from parent varieties Kidd's Orange and Golden Delicious, this apple is pale to golden yellow with red stripes or blush. Its flavor is sweet and aromatic, and it has a firm, crisp texture. Galas are recommended for fresh eating and for applesauce and desserts.

Braeburn: Discovered as a chance seedling in New Zealand in 1952, Braeburn is believed to be a cross between Granny Smith and Lady Hamilton. The color ranges from red blush on a green background to all red. The flavor is mildly sweet/tart, with intense flavor and good aromatics. Firm, crisp, and juicy, Braeburn is recommended for eating fresh as well as for cooking.

Jonagold: This cross between Golden Delicious and Jonathan was developed in New York in the 1960s. The round to conical fruit is bright red over gold, has a moderately sweet/tart flavor, and is firm and crisp. Jonagold is wonderful in salads and for cooking and baking.

Other varieties sometimes found in Northwest markets include Gravenstein (a crisp, acidic early-ripening older variety) and Spartan (a cross between McIntosh and Yellow Newtown Pippin).

SPINACH SALAD

Delilah's, Vancouver, British Columbia

At Delilah's they top this piquant salad with grilled peppers
just before serving. You can also use roasted bell peppers from a jar, or
fresh bell peppers, as we do here. Filled with beans, feta cheese, and fried
pancetta, the salad is hearty enough to be served as a main dish.

1 bunch spinach, tough stems removed | *2 tablespoons pine nuts, toasted*
½ cup cooked white beans | *2 tablespoons diced pancetta or bacon*
(canned or freshly cooked) | *¼ red bell pepper, cored, seeded, and diced*
2 tablespoons crumbled feta cheese | *¼ yellow bell pepper, cored, seeded, and diced*

BALSAMIC VINAIGRETTE

⅓ cup olive oil | *½ teaspoon Dijon-style mustard*
2 tablespoons balsamic vinegar | *Salt and freshly ground black pepper*
1½ teaspoons minced basil |

FOR THE VINAIGRETTE, combine the oil, vinegar, basil, and mustard in a small bowl
and whisk to mix. Add salt and pepper to taste and set aside.

FRY THE PANCETTA in a small skillet until crisp. In a large bowl, combine the
spinach, beans, feta, pine nuts, pancetta, and bell peppers. Drizzle the vinaigrette over
the salad and toss to mix well. Arrange the salad on individual plates, distributing the
ingredients as evenly as possible. Serve immediately.

Makes 4 servings

WARM BEAN SALAD WITH LAMB

Christina's, Orcas Island, Washington

Tossed with winter greens, this nourishing salad makes a delicious lunch or dinner, especially served with a glass of velvety-rich Hogue Cellars merlot. This is a great use of leftover lamb—or substitute chicken, duck, or roast beef.

1¼ cups dry beans, preferably appaloosa, chestnut, cannellini, or other heritage beans
1 red bell pepper
1 small red onion, halved and thinly sliced
1 fennel bulb, trimmed, cored, and thinly sliced

¾ pound cooked lamb, shredded
4 to 6 cups mixed winter greens (arugula, frisée, escarole), torn into large pieces
Radicchio and sage leaves, for garnish

VINAIGRETTE

⅓ cup sherry vinegar
1 clove garlic, minced
1 teaspoon thyme leaves
1 teaspoon chopped chives

1 teaspoon minced sage
1 cup pure olive oil (not extra-virgin)
Salt and freshly ground black pepper

PUT THE BEANS in a large bowl and pour boiling water over to cover them by 1 inch. Let sit for 1 hour, then drain the beans and put them in a saucepan with fresh, cold water to cover by 2 inches. Bring to a boil, reduce the heat, and simmer until the beans are tender, about 30 minutes, adding more boiling water if necessary to keep the beans completely covered. Drain the beans and set aside.

FOR THE VINAIGRETTE, whisk together the vinegar, garlic, thyme, chives, and sage. Whisk in the olive oil and season to taste with salt and pepper. Set aside.

ROAST THE RED PEPPER over a gas flame or under the broiler, turning often, until evenly charred. Put the pepper in a paper or plastic bag, close the bag, and let sit until cool enough to handle. Remove the skin, then halve the pepper, discarding the core and seeds. Cut the pepper into thin strips and set aside.

PREHEAT THE OVEN to 400°F.

COMBINE THE BEANS, roasted bell pepper, onion, fennel, and lamb in a large stainless steel bowl. Whisk the vinaigrette to remix and pour about ½ cup of it over the bean mixture. Toss to mix, then put the bowl in the oven 8 to 12 minutes.

REMOVE THE BOWL from the oven, add the greens, and toss until they are mixed into the salad and have wilted. Taste the salad for seasoning, adding more dressing, salt, or pepper to taste. Immediately arrange the salad on individual plates, with the greens toward the bottom and other ingredients on top. Garnish the plates with radicchio and sage leaves and serve immediately.

Makes 4 to 6 servings

FRISÉE WITH RED BEETS
and Blue Cheese

Marco's Supperclub, Seattle, Washington

No food smacks of the sweet earth more than tender cooked beets. Here they're combined with slightly bitter frisée greens and tangy blue cheese. For best results, wrap the beet in foil and roast in a 400°F oven for about 1 hour, or until tender. You can also boil the beet for about 30 minutes. When frisée isn't available, this salad is also delicious made with escarole or romaine lettuce.

1 cooked medium red beet (about 10 ounces), peeled, trimmed, and cut in julienne strips
1 tablespoon cider vinegar
1 tablespoon minced mint
2 teaspoons minced shallots

2 teaspoons sugar
Salt and freshly ground black pepper
1 or 2 heads baby frisée greens, rinsed and torn into large pieces
¼ cup crumbled blue cheese, or more to taste

SHERRY VINAIGRETTE

2 tablespoons pure olive oil
1 tablespoon extra-virgin olive oil
1 tablespoon sherry vinegar

1 teaspoon minced shallots
1 teaspoon Dijon-style mustard
1 teaspoon minced thyme

COMBINE THE BEETS, vinegar, mint, shallots, and sugar with a pinch each of salt and pepper in a bowl and toss to mix well. Set aside for 1 hour, or cover and refrigerate for up to 1 day.

FOR THE VINAIGRETTE, combine the oils, vinegar, shallots, mustard, and thyme in a small bowl and whisk to mix. Season to taste with salt and pepper.

COMBINE THE FRISÉE and beets in a large bowl. Pour the vinaigrette over the salad and toss to mix well. Arrange on individual plates, sprinkle the blue cheese over the salad, and serve.

Makes 4 servings

HEARTS OF ROMAINE WITH CHICKEN
and Warm Asian Ginger Sauce

Kaspar's, Seattle, Washington

Light and flavorful, this elegant salad from chef Kaspar Donier is perfect for a spring dinner. If possible, use Momokawa sake, an outstanding product imported from Japan by way of Oregon, in the recipe. A glass of their premium Gold Label Sake, served chilled, makes a delicious accompaniment.

1 large head romaine lettuce
1 boneless, skinless chicken breast, cut in thin strips (about 6 ounces)
Salt and freshly ground black pepper
1 teaspoon vegetable oil
½ cup chicken stock (see page 81)
¼ cup sake or sweet white wine

1 tablespoon oyster sauce
1 tablespoon seasoned rice vinegar
1 teaspoon chopped ginger
1 teaspoon soy sauce
½ teaspoon chopped garlic
1 green onion, thinly sliced
½ teaspoon toasted sesame seeds

DISCARD THE TOUGH outer leaves from the romaine and cut away the core. Cut the romaine lengthwise into quarters, rinse, and dry well. Chill until needed.

SEASON THE CHICKEN strips lightly with salt and pepper. Heat the oil in a large skillet, preferably nonstick, over medium-high heat. Add the chicken strips and cook until well browned on all sides, 3 to 4 minutes. Add the chicken stock, sake, oyster sauce, vinegar, ginger, soy sauce, and garlic. Cook over medium heat until slightly thickened, about 5 minutes. Taste for seasoning.

PLACE THE ROMAINE quarters on individual plates. Spoon the chicken and sauce over and around the romaine. Sprinkle the green onion and sesame seeds over the salad. Serve immediately.

Makes 2 to 4 servings

INDONESIAN RICE SALAD

The Bagelry, Bellingham, Washington

Topped with a zesty ginger and citrus dressing, this substantial salad, packed with raisins, water chestnuts, and cashews, can stand on its own as an entrée.

4½ cups water

2 cups long-grain rice, such as basmati or jasmine

1½ cups mung bean sprouts

1 bunch green onions, trimmed and sliced

1 red bell pepper, cored, seeded, and chopped

1 green bell pepper, cored, seeded, and chopped

¾ cup toasted coconut

¾ cup raisins

1 can (5½ ounces) sliced water chestnuts, drained

½ cup cashews

⅓ cup sesame seeds

DRESSING

½ cup freshly squeezed orange juice

¼ cup vegetable oil

¼ cup soy sauce

3 tablespoons freshly squeezed lemon juice

2 tablespoons honey

1½ tablespoons sesame oil

3 to 5 cloves garlic, minced

1 teaspoon powdered ginger

Salt and freshly ground black pepper

BRING THE WATER to a boil, stir in the rice, and return just to a boil. Lower the heat, cover the pan, and simmer until the rice is tender and all the water is absorbed, about 20 minutes. When cooked, transfer the rice to a large bowl.

FOR THE DRESSING, stir together the orange juice, vegetable oil, soy sauce, lemon juice, honey, sesame oil, garlic, and ginger in a small bowl. Season to taste with salt and pepper. Pour the dressing over the warm rice and toss gently until well mixed. Refrigerate until thoroughly chilled, about 2 hours.

WHEN THE RICE is chilled, add the bean sprouts, green onions, bell peppers, coconut, raisins, water chestnuts, cashews, and sesame seeds. Toss well. Taste for seasoning and serve.

Makes 6 to 8 servings

TOMATO CHEDDAR DILL BREAD

Abigail's Hotel, Victoria, British Columbia

Abigail's serves this beautiful, tangy bread for breakfast. You'll
get the accolades if you offer it at your next brunch.

2 cups all-purpose flour
1 cup grated cheddar cheese
1½ teaspoons baking powder
1 teaspoon salt
½ teaspoon baking soda
1 cup puréed tomato (fresh or canned)

¾ cup minced onion
¼ cup minced fresh dill,
* or 1 tablespoon dried*
¼ cup vegetable oil
2 eggs

PREHEAT THE OVEN to 375°F. Lightly grease a 5- by 9-inch loaf pan.

STIR TOGETHER the flour, cheese, baking powder, salt, and baking soda in a large
bowl. In another bowl, combine the tomato purée, onion, dill, oil, and eggs. Add this
mixture to the dry ingredients and stir just until thoroughly blended. Pour the batter
into the loaf pan and bake until bread is nicely browned and a toothpick inserted in
the center comes out clean, 50 to 55 minutes. Turn the bread onto a wire rack to cool
before cutting.

Makes 1 loaf

HAZELNUT AND ONION BREAD

Columbia Gorge Hotel, Hood River, Oregon

Flavored with onions and hazelnuts, this savory loaf is delicious spread with butter, or served with local cheeses and a glass of Oregon pinot noir.

3 cups bread flour	1½ teaspoons salt
½ cup chopped toasted hazelnuts	¾ teaspoon sugar
3 tablespoons canola oil	1½ tablespoons (1½ packages)
¼ cup finely chopped onion	active dry yeast
2 teaspoons onion powder	1 cup warm water

COMBINE THE FLOUR, hazelnuts, oil, onion, onion powder, salt, and sugar in the large bowl of an electric mixer and stir. Sprinkle the yeast over the warm water in a small bowl and let sit until yeast dissolves and mixture begins to bubble, 2 to 3 minutes. Pour the water and yeast mixture into the flour mixture and mix with a dough hook until thoroughly combined, about 6 minutes. Continue kneading the dough until smooth and supple, a few minutes longer. Place the dough in a lightly oiled bowl, cover with a warm, damp cloth, and let rise in a warm place until doubled in bulk, about 1 hour.

PUT THE DOUGH on a lightly floured work surface. Flatten the dough into a rectangle, removing all air bubbles. Roll the dough tightly into a cylinder. Use your hands to gently taper and round the ends; the loaf should have an elongated, oval shape. Place the loaf on a baking sheet, seam side down, and let rise until doubled, about 1 hour longer.

PREHEAT THE OVEN to 350°F.

JUST BEFORE BAKING, make a shallow lengthwise slit in the top of the loaf with a sharp knife. Brush the loaf with water and bake until the bread is nicely browned, about 40 minutes.

Makes 1 loaf

In Europe the hazelnut is also called the filbert or the cobnut. The former name honors St. Philibert, a seventh-century abbot whose feast day, August 22, falls when the nuts are ripening. In the United States, some people call them hazelnuts and other call them filberts. Whatever name you choose for them, they are a delicacy.

Ninety-eight percent of the hazelnuts raised in the United States are grown in Oregon's Willamette Valley; the other 2 percent come from southwestern Washington. Oregon hazelnuts, which make up 3 percent of the world's production, are renowned for their extremely large size and exceptional flavor. An English sailor planted the first cultivated hazelnut tree in 1858 in Oregon's Umpqua Valley. The tree still stands today.

Hazelnuts are harvested in the fall, when the air is brisk and the leaves dazzle the eye. These bushy shrubs and trees are native to the temperate regions of the Northern Hemisphere, including Europe and the Pacific Northwest. Because the nuts of the wild hazels indigenous to the Pacific Northwest are quite small, the hazelnuts favored for cultivation are European species. The three hazelnut varieties raised commercially in Oregon are Barcelona (the most common variety), Ennis, and Daviana.

Like all nuts, hazelnuts are a good source of B vitamins, protein, fat, and fiber; they are especially rich in vitamin E, copper, and magnesium. Roasted hazelnuts have an alluring, sweet, toasty aroma; a buttery, rich flavor; and an addictive crunch.

TO TOAST HAZELNUTS AND OTHER NUTS

Preheat the oven to 350°F. Distribute shelled nuts evenly over a baking pan in a single layer. Roast in the oven, stirring occasionally, until the nuts are golden brown and fragrant. The time needed will depend on the size and variety of the nut. Most nuts will toast in about 10 minutes. Smaller nuts, or small pieces, will toast more quickly. Over-toasting will give nuts an unpleasant bitter flavor.

To remove the papery skins from roasted hazelnuts, gather the nuts in a dish towel and rub briskly between layers of towel.

OREGON HONEY-HAZELNUT WHOLE WHEAT BREAD

Canyon Way Restaurant and Bookstore, Newport, Oregon

Canyon Way bakes this coastal favorite every day. It's best served warm from the oven, slathered with sweet butter. Or try it with apples and sharp cheese.

2 cups all-purpose flour	*1 tablespoon (1 package) rapid-rise yeast*
2 cups coarse whole wheat flour (graham flour)	*2 teaspoons salt*
½ cup toasted, finely chopped hazelnuts	*2 cups warm water*
¼ cup honey	*1 to 1½ cups fine whole wheat flour*
2 tablespoons butter, softened	

COMBINE THE ALL-PURPOSE flour and the coarse whole wheat flour in a large bowl. Stir in the hazelnuts, honey, butter, yeast, and salt. Gradually add the warm water, stirring well to incorporate. Stir in 1 cup of the fine whole wheat flour until well mixed, then add enough of the remaining flour to form a smooth and moist, but not sticky, dough. Knead the dough for a few minutes, then cover it with a damp cloth and let rise in a warm place until doubled in bulk, about 1½ hours.

PUNCH DOWN THE DOUGH and knead to remove as much air as possible. Cut the dough in half and gently form each half into a round about 6 inches across. Set the rounds on a lightly greased baking sheet. Make shallow slashes in the top of each round. Cover the loaves with a cloth and let rise for 20 to 30 minutes longer.

PREHEAT THE OVEN to 400°F.

BAKE until the bread is nicely browned and a loaf sounds hollow when tapped on the bottom, 25 to 30 minutes. Transfer to a wire rack to cool.

Makes 2 loaves

FAIRBURN PEASANT BREAD

Fairburn Farm Country Manor, Duncan, British Columbia

They grow and grind their own wheat at the Fairburn Farm Country Manor, an organic farm since 1955. Brimming with the nutty sweetness of fresh whole wheat flour and rolled oats, this hearty bread is great with soup or cheese.

¾ teaspoon sugar	2 teaspoons molasses
2⅔ cups lukewarm water	2 teaspoons salt
1½ tablespoons (1½ packages)	1⅓ cups rolled oats, plus more for pans
active dry yeast	6 to 7 cups whole wheat flour, or half
⅓ cup butter, melted, or vegetable oil	whole wheat flour and half unbleached
⅓ cup packed brown sugar or honey	all-purpose flour

DISSOLVE THE SUGAR in 1 cup of the lukewarm water in a large bowl and sprinkle the yeast over it. Let sit until bubbly, 5 to 10 minutes, then stir to mix well. Add the remaining 1⅔ cups water with the melted butter or oil, brown sugar, molasses, and salt; stir to mix. Stir in the oats, followed by the flour, 1 cup at a time. When the dough is firm, turn it onto a lightly floured work surface and knead until it is smooth and supple, about 10 minutes. Put the dough in a lightly oiled bowl, turning to evenly coat it in oil. Cover with a cloth and let rise in a warm place until doubled in bulk, about 1½ hours.

TURN THE DOUGH OUT onto a lightly oiled surface and punch it down. Grease two 5- by 9-inch loaf pans and sprinkle the insides sparingly with some oats. Divide the dough in half and shape each into a cylinder that fits snugly in the pan. Put the loaves in the pans, cover with a cloth, and let rise in a warm place until doubled and the loaf tops are rounded and smooth, about 1 hour.

PREHEAT THE OVEN to 400°F. Bake the loaves for 20 minutes, reduce the heat to 350°F, and continue baking until the loaves are browned, 15 to 20 minutes longer. To check for doneness, tip one loaf carefully from the pan and tap the bottom of the loaf with your fingers; it should sound hollow. Turn the loaves out onto a wire rack to cool, with a cloth over them to help keep the crust soft.

Makes 2 loaves

LEMON THYME ZUCCHINI BREAD

Chateau Whistler Resort, Whistler, British Columbia

Here's a zucchini loaf delicately perfumed with fresh lemon thyme. It's ideal with an afternoon cup of tea or coffee. Lemon thyme, a tiny perennial herbaceous shrub of the mint family, grows extremely well in the Pacific Northwest. With its colorful variegated foliage, it makes a lovely addition to a windowbox or garden.

3 cups all-purpose flour
¾ cup raisins
1 tablespoon ground cinnamon
1 teaspoon ground nutmeg
1 teaspoon baking soda
1 teaspoon baking powder
½ teaspoon salt
2 whole eggs, or 4 egg whites
1 cup packed brown sugar

¾ cup plain lowfat yogurt
⅓ cup vegetable oil
¼ cup milk
2 teaspoons vanilla extract
2 cups finely grated unpeeled zucchini
  (about 1 medium zucchini)
Leaves from 2 bunches lemon thyme
  (about ½ cup)

PREHEAT THE OVEN to 350°F. Lightly grease a 5- by 9-inch loaf pan.

STIR TOGETHER the flour, raisins, cinnamon, nutmeg, baking soda, baking powder, and salt. In a large bowl, whip the eggs or egg whites until frothy, then stir in the brown sugar, yogurt, oil, milk, and vanilla. Stir in the zucchini and lemon thyme.

ADD THE DRY ingredients to the zucchini mixture and stir gently just until thoroughly combined. Pour the batter into the prepared loaf pan and bake until a toothpick inserted in the center comes out clean, 55 to 65 minutes. Turn the bread onto a wire rack and let cool before slicing.

Makes 1 loaf

MAIN DISHES

POULET AUX CREVETTES
(Chicken with Shrimp)

Charles at Smugglers Cove, Mukilteo, Washington

Exciting tales of bootlegging and smuggling surround this
restaurant, which was formerly a speakeasy and distillery built in 1929. Today,
the excitement here lies in Northwest ingredients cooked in traditional French
ways. This innovative take on a classic chicken dish is made with a sauce composed
of shrimp, cream, tomatoes, and white wine. Serve with steamed rice.

4 boneless, skinless chicken breasts	*½ cup diced tomato*
(about 6 ounces each)	*½ cup dry white wine*
Salt and freshly ground black pepper	*½ cup whipping cream*
¼ cup all-purpose flour	*2 shallots, minced*
2 tablespoons butter	*2 cloves garlic, minced*
4 ounces medium shrimp, peeled and deveined	*2 tablespoons minced flat-leaf (Italian) parsley*

PREHEAT THE OVEN to 375°F.

LIGHTLY SEASON the chicken breasts with salt and pepper. Coat each in flour, patting
to remove excess. Heat the butter in a sauté pan or ovenproof skillet, add the chicken
breasts, and cook over medium-high heat until well browned, 2 to 3 minutes on each
side. Spoon off and discard excess butter from the pan; add the shrimp, tomato, wine,
cream, shallots, and garlic. Put the pan in the oven and bake until the chicken is just
cooked through, about 15 minutes. Transfer the chicken to individual warmed plates
and season the sauce to taste with salt and pepper. Spoon the shrimp and sauce over
the chicken, sprinkle each plate with parsley, and serve immediately.

Makes 4 servings

CHICKEN IN PAPRIKA-LACED WALNUT SAUCE

Cafe Langley, Langley, Washington

This aromatic dish is very popular throughout the Mediterranean, particularly in Turkey, where it is called Circassian chicken. Be sure to use fresh, sweet walnuts and top-quality paprika. Rice pilaf or risotto (cooked in some of the chicken stock) goes well with this dish.

½ cup chopped onion	7 black peppercorns
½ cup chopped carrot	Pinch salt
5 sprigs flat-leaf (Italian) parsley	8 cups water
2 bay leaves	1 whole chicken, cut in half or quarters

PAPRIKA OIL

3 tablespoons walnut oil	2 teaspoons sweet paprika, preferably Hungarian

WALNUT SAUCE

2 or 3 slices French bread (about 2 ounces), crusts removed	2 tablespoons sweet paprika, preferably Hungarian
½ cup milk	1½ tablespoons minced garlic
¾ pound walnut pieces (about 3 cups)	¼ teaspoon cayenne pepper
⅓ cup minced onion	Salt and freshly ground black pepper
	½ cup walnut halves, for garnish

PUT THE ONION, carrot, parsley, bay leaves, peppercorns, and salt in a large pot with the water. Bring to a boil and simmer gently for 20 minutes. Add the chicken pieces, with more hot water if needed to fully cover the chicken, and simmer until the meat is just cooked through, 20 to 30 minutes. Let the chicken cool in the stock. When cool enough to handle, discard the skin from the chicken and pull all the meat from the bones. Break the meat into bite-sized pieces and set aside. Strain the stock and let sit until settled, about 15 minutes. Skim excess fat from the top with a large spoon, and set the stock aside.

FOR THE PAPRIKA OIL, heat the walnut oil in a small pan until just warm. Stir in the paprika and let sit to infuse in a warm spot on the stove.

FOR THE WALNUT SAUCE, put the bread in a small dish, pour the milk over, and let soak until soft. Squeeze the bread dry, discarding the milk, and set aside. Grind the walnuts in a food processor or blender until finely chopped, then put them in a large saucepan. Crumble the bread into the pan, then add the onion, paprika, garlic, cayenne, and 2 cups of the chicken stock. Bring to a boil, stirring constantly. Reduce the heat and simmer for 3 to 5 minutes. Season to taste with salt and pepper. If necessary, add a little more chicken stock to make a thick pouring consistency.

COMBINE HALF OF THE SAUCE with the reserved chicken meat and arrange it on a serving platter. Spoon the remaining sauce over the chicken and garnish with the walnut halves. Drizzle the paprika oil over all and serve at room temperature or chilled.

Makes 4 servings

HAZELNUT CHICKEN BREASTS
with Berry Sauce

Giraffe Restaurant, White Rock, British Columbia

Chef/owner Corinne Poole dreamed up this Northwest dish while sitting on a beach in Hawaii, feeling homesick for British Columbia. At the restaurant, she serves it with grilled asparagus drizzled with a balsamic vinaigrette.

4 boneless, skinless chicken breasts
(about 6 ounces each)
1 tablespoon Dijon-style mustard
2 teaspoons minced fresh herbs (such as
marjoram, oregano, thyme, and parsley)

Salt and freshly ground black pepper
1 cup all-purpose flour
1 egg
2 tablespoons milk
1 cup coarsely ground hazelnuts

BERRY SAUCE

1 cup blackberries
(fresh or unsweetened frozen)
1 cup raspberries (fresh or unsweetened frozen)
½ cup water
2 shallots, minced

3 tablespoons raspberry vinegar
or red wine vinegar
3 tablespoons crème de cassis
(black currant liqueur) (optional)
1 tablespoon sugar

LAY THE CHICKEN BREASTS in a dish and spread them evenly with mustard. Sprinkle the herbs over them, season with pepper, cover, and refrigerate for at least 1 hour.

FOR THE BERRY SAUCE, combine the berries, water, shallots, vinegar, crème de cassis (if using), and sugar in a medium-sized, heavy saucepan. Bring just to a boil; reduce the heat and simmer, stirring often, until the mixture is well blended and thick, 12 to 15 minutes. Season to taste with salt and pepper. If you prefer a very smooth sauce, purée it in a food processor and pass through a sieve back into the pan. Keep warm.

PREHEAT THE OVEN to 450°F.

PUT THE FLOUR in a shallow dish and season liberally with salt and pepper. In another shallow dish, lightly beat the egg and milk. Put the ground hazelnuts in a third dish.

DIP A CHICKEN BREAST in the flour to coat, patting to remove excess flour. Dip the breast in the beaten egg, allow excess to drip off, then coat the breast evenly with the hazelnuts. Set the breast on a lightly greased baking sheet and repeat with the remaining chicken breasts.

BAKE THE CHICKEN until cooked through, 12 to 15 minutes. Arrange each breast on an individual plate, drizzle some of the berry sauce over and around it, and serve immediately.

Makes 4 servings

THAI MINT NOODLES

Passport, Everett, Washington

Smothered in a creamy peanut sauce, tender chunks of chicken, shrimp, and crisp vegetables are blended with silky rice noodles to create the Passport's most popular dish. Although most of the ingredients can be found in grocery stores, you may need to seek out a store that specializes in Thai ingredients to find kaffir lime leaves and lemongrass. If available, use fresh rice noodles in place of dried.

½ pound dry rice noodles	*1 red bell pepper, cored, seeded,*
¼ cup vegetable oil	*and thinly sliced*
⅓ pound shrimp, peeled and deveined	*4 ounces mushrooms, thinly sliced*
1 boneless, skinless chicken breast (about 6	*2 cups broccoli florets (about 4 ounces)*
ounces), cut in thin strips	*1 large carrot, thinly sliced*
2 bok choy leaves, thinly sliced	*½ cup coarsely chopped mint leaves*
(about 2½ cups)	*1 tablespoon minced or grated ginger*
	1 clove garlic, minced

THAI NOODLE SAUCE

2 tablespoons oil	*1 cup unsweetened coconut milk*
1 cup chopped onion	*1 cup chunky peanut butter*
2 cloves garlic, minced	*½ cup milk*
1 tablespoon chopped lemongrass,	*1 cinnamon stick, 2 inches long*
or 1 tablespoon lemon juice	*3 bay leaves*
3 kaffir lime leaves, or 2 teaspoons	*3 tablespoons bottled Asian fish sauce*
grated lime zest	*3 tablespoons packed brown sugar*
1 teaspoon Thai curry paste, or 1 teaspoon	*3 tablespoons freshly squeezed lemon juice*
minced fresh chile	*2 teaspoons tamarind paste, or 1 tablespoon*
½ teaspoon curry powder	*freshly squeezed lime juice*

NUOC CHAM

¼ cup rice vinegar	2 tablespoons freshly squeezed lime juice
¼ cup bottled Asian fish sauce (nam pla)	2 teaspoons minced garlic
¼ cup water	1 small Thai bird chile, sliced,
2 tablespoons granulated sugar	or 1 whole dried chile

SOAK THE RICE NOODLES in hot water until soft, 20 to 30 minutes. Drain very well and pat dry on paper towels.

FOR THE THAI NOODLE SAUCE, heat the oil in a medium saucepan. Add the onion, garlic, lemongrass, lime leaves, curry paste, and curry powder and sauté for 2 minutes. Stir in the coconut milk, peanut butter, regular milk, cinnamon stick, bay leaves, fish sauce, brown sugar, lemon juice, and tamarind paste. Mix well and set aside; the sauce will thicken as it cools.

FOR THE NUOC CHAM, combine the vinegar, fish sauce, water, sugar, lime juice, garlic, and chile in a small saucepan. Bring to a boil and stir just until the sugar has dissolved. Set aside.

HEAT 1 TABLESPOON of the oil in a large wok or heavy skillet over medium-high heat. When hot, add the noodles and stir-fry for 2 minutes. Transfer the noodles to a large bowl and set aside. Heat another tablespoon of oil in the pan, add the shrimp and chicken, and stir-fry until just cooked through, 3 to 5 minutes. Transfer to the bowl with the noodles.

HEAT ANOTHER TABLESPOON of oil in the pan and add the bok choy, bell pepper, mushrooms, broccoli, and carrot. Stir-fry until the vegetables are just crisp-tender, about 3 minutes. Add the mint leaves, ginger, and garlic along with the nuoc cham and Thai noodle sauce and stir to mix. Add the noodles, shrimp, and chicken. Stir until heated through, about 1 minute. Serve immediately.

Makes 4 to 6 servings

HERBAL TEA-SMOKED CHICKEN BREAST

The Sutton Place Hotel, Vancouver, British Columbia

Infused with the smoky essence of herbal tea leaves, these grilled chicken breasts are napped with a fruity blueberry sauce. Chef Louis Gervais uses a Sutton Place house blend herbal tea, but any herbal tea blend works well. The sauce gets body from demi-glace, a rich, concentrated stock that some stores sell in small disks. You may prefer to use a good chicken stock, but reduce it by half before adding the blueberries.

4 chicken breasts (with bone still in), preferably grain-fed (about 8 ounces each)	1 shallot, minced
1 tablespoon coarse salt	¼ cup dry red wine
2 ounces herbal tea leaves (about 1½ cups)	1 cup demi-glace or reduced chicken stock
½ cup butter	1 cup blueberries
	Salt and freshly ground black pepper

PUT THE CHICKEN in a shallow dish, sprinkle the coarse salt over it, and marinate in the refrigerator for 2 hours. Rinse off the salt and pat dry with paper towels.

PREHEAT AN OUTDOOR GRILL with a moderate fire. Soak the tea leaves in a bowl of warm tap water for 30 minutes. When the coals are hot, drain the tea leaves well and sprinkle them over the coals. Set the chicken on the grate, cover the grill, and smoke the chicken, without turning, until it is just cooked through, 20 to 30 minutes.

WHILE THE CHICKEN is smoking, prepare the sauce. Heat 2 tablespoons of the butter in a medium saucepan until melted (chill the remaining butter). Add the shallot and cook over medium heat until softened, 2 to 3 minutes. Add the wine, bring to a boil, and boil until reduced by about half. Add the demi-glace and blueberries and simmer gently for 15 minutes. Cut the remaining butter into chunks, add it to the sauce, and stir so the butter melts gently into the sauce without separating. Season to taste with salt and pepper.

SET A CHICKEN BREAST on each individual plate and drizzle the sauce over and around it. Serve immediately.

Makes 4 servings

ROTINI WITH SEARED QUAIL BREAST,
Porcini Mushrooms, and Sage

CinCin, Vancouver, British Columbia

The integrity of this wintry pasta dish depends on the flavor of dried porcini mushrooms, which are much more flavorful than fresh ones. Shortly beforehand, put them in a small bowl and soak in hot water to soften.

1 to 2 ounces dried porcini mushrooms	*1 cup quail or chicken stock*
½ cup hot water (more if needed)	*(use remaining portions of quail)*
12 ounces dried rotini pasta	*3 tablespoons minced sage*
2 tablespoons vegetable oil	*Pinch dried red pepper flakes*
8 whole, boned quail breasts	*1 tablespoon butter, chilled*
¼ cup minced shallot or onion	*Salt and freshly ground black pepper*
1 tablespoon minced garlic	*¼ cup grated Parmesan or Romano cheese*

BRING A LARGE PAN of lightly salted water to a boil, add the pasta, and simmer until al dente, 7 to 10 minutes. Drain well, toss in 1 tablespoon of the oil, and set aside.

HEAT THE REMAINING 1 tablespoon oil in a large, heavy skillet over medium-high heat. When hot, add the quail breasts and sear until nicely browned on each side but still rare, 1 to 2 minutes per side. Set aside. Add the shallot and garlic to the skillet and cook over medium heat until just tender and fragrant, 2 to 3 minutes.

MEANWHILE, DRAIN THE MUSHROOMS, reserving the liquid. Coarsely chop the mushrooms and add them to the skillet with their liquid. Bring to a boil and boil until the liquid is reduced to about 2 tablespoons. Add the stock and boil until reduced by about half. Add the quail breasts with the sage and red pepper flakes. Cook gently, stirring, until the quail is heated through, 2 to 3 minutes. Remove the skillet from the heat and add the butter, stirring until melted. Add the pasta and salt and pepper to taste, tossing to mix well. Divide the pasta among 4 individual plates, with 2 quail breasts on each plate. Sprinkle the grated cheese over all and serve immediately.

Makes 4 servings

FOREST CHICKEN

Sol Duc Hot Springs, Port Angeles, Washington

Sol Duc chef Mike Rogers features this seductive recipe each fall, when local apples and wild mushrooms are abundant. Apricot-scented chanterelles are the chef's favorite, but morels, shiitakes, oyster mushrooms, or portobellos can all be used. Columbia Winery's smoky, earthy Red Willow Vineyard Syrah marries exceptionally well with this woodsy dish.

½ cup all-purpose flour
Salt and freshly ground black pepper
4 chicken breasts, bone still in
(about 8 ounces each)
¼ cup olive oil
2 teaspoons chopped garlic
2 teaspoons minced shallot
8 ounces wild mushrooms, cleaned, trimmed, and sliced

½ cup veal or chicken stock
⅓ cup diced tart apple, such as Granny Smith or Gravenstein
¼ cup chopped walnuts
2 tablespoons dry sherry
2 tablespoons dry white wine
2 teaspoons minced tarragon
1 teaspoon minced thyme

PREHEAT THE OVEN to 350°F.

SEASON THE FLOUR with a generous pinch each of salt and pepper. Dust the chicken with the seasoned flour, patting to remove excess. In a large skillet, heat the oil over medium-high heat. Add the chicken and sauté until golden brown, 3 to 4 minutes per side. Remove the chicken from the pan and set it in a shallow baking dish. Bake the chicken until it is no longer pink in the center of the thickest part, 15 to 20 minutes.

PREPARE THE SAUCE while the chicken is baking. Pour off all but about 1 table-spoon of the oil from the pan the chicken was cooked in, and reheat the pan over medium-high heat. Add the garlic and shallot and sauté for 1 minute. Add the mush-rooms and cook until just tender, about 3 minutes. Add the stock, apple, walnuts, sherry, white wine, tarragon, and thyme. Cook, stirring occasionally, until reduced by about half. Taste the sauce for seasoning, adding salt and pepper to taste.

ARRANGE THE CHICKEN breasts on individual plates, pour the sauce over them, and serve immediately.

Makes 4 servings

WILD NORTHWEST MUSHROOMS

With its mild, damp climate and rich woodland soils, the Pacific Northwest is a mushroom collectors' paradise. The region is also home to two species of truffles—the Oregon white and the Oregon black truffles. The following mushrooms grow wild in the Northwest; they are also commonly available in local markets. Because some wild mushrooms are highly toxic, you should consult an expert if you don't know how to identify them, or purchase them from a reputable market.

Oyster mushroom: Pale-gray to beige, oyster mushrooms, with their frilly, oyster shell–shaped caps, have a delicate woodsy flavor with a hint of anise.

Boletus: Also known as *porcini* or *cèpes*, these golden-brown members of the *Boletus edulis* species are thick and meaty, with deep, intense flavor. They have bulbous stems and big, round caps that can stretch 8 inches across. Boletus are often sold dried.

Chanterelle: Wild golden chanterelles, with their delicate apricot scent and sweet, earthy flavor, are a favorite with Northwest cooks. Shaped like an umbrella that's been folded inside-out, chanterelles are harvested wild in the spring and fall. White and black chanterelles also grow wild in the Northwest, and the black chanterelle is cultivated locally on a small scale.

Morel: Sweet and earthy, with a delicious caramel flavor when sautéed, morels are harvested wild each spring and may soon become available commercially. They are frequently sold dried. Brown and shaped like pine cones, morels have a chambered outer flesh that resembles sponge or coral.

Matsutake: Highly favored in Asian cooking, matsutake mushrooms have a pungent, spicy aroma similar to horseradish. They grow beneath Northwest pine trees, and are harvested in the fall. These brown-gilled mushrooms have a cream- to beige-colored, 3- to 5-inch cap and stem.

ASIAN DUCK CONFIT
with Shiitake Mushroom Couscous

Kaspar's, Seattle, Washington

In a heated competition held at the prestigious James Beard
House in Manhattan, chef Kaspar Donier was proclaimed the national winner of
the 1995 Evian Healthy Menu Awards with this flavorful dish. After removing the
leg thigh portions, use the duck carcasses for some fabulous stock and the
breasts for another dish. Accompany the meal with a Paul Thomas
cabernet-merlot and you've got a winning combination.

4 duck leg/thigh portions	*½ stalk lemongrass, coarsely chopped*
4 cups water	*3 tablespoons oyster sauce*
1 cup dry sherry	*2 tablespoons coarsely chopped ginger*
1 medium onion, coarsely chopped	*1 tablespoon sesame oil*
¼ cup honey	*3 cloves garlic, crushed*
¼ cup soy sauce	*1 teaspoon dried red pepper flakes*
3 green onions, coarsely chopped	

SHIITAKE MUSHROOM COUSCOUS

1 tablespoon olive oil	*1¾ cups chicken stock (see page 81)*
1 large leek, trimmed, washed,	*1 cup whole wheat couscous*
and cut in julienne strips	*Salt*
½ pound shiitake mushrooms, cleaned,	
trimmed, and thinly sliced	

TRIM EXCESS FAT from the duck legs.

COMBINE THE WATER, sherry, onion, honey, soy sauce, green onions, lemongrass,
oyster sauce, ginger, sesame oil, garlic, and red pepper flakes in a large pot and bring to a
boil. Add the duck legs and return to a boil. Reduce the heat and simmer until the duck
is very tender, about 1½ hours.

REMOVE THE DUCK from the broth with a slotted spoon and let cool slightly. Remove and discard the skin; cover to keep warm. Using a large spoon, skim off and discard the fat that has risen to the top of the broth. Strain the broth into a smaller saucepan and boil until reduced by about half, about 20 minutes.

PREPARE THE COUSCOUS while the broth is reducing. Heat the oil in a medium saucepan over medium heat. Add the leek and cook, stirring, until it softens and begins to brown, 2 to 3 minutes. Add the mushrooms and continue cooking until they are tender and begin to give off their liquid, 3 to 4 minutes longer.

ADD THE CHICKEN STOCK and bring to a boil. Stir in the couscous, remove the pan from the heat, cover, and let sit until the liquid has been absorbed and the couscous is tender, about 5 minutes. Season to taste with salt. Keep warm.

RETURN THE DUCK LEGS to the broth and reheat for a few minutes. Spoon the couscous onto individual plates and top each serving with a duck leg. Spoon some of the reduced cooking liquid over the duck and couscous and serve.

Makes 4 servings

STORING FRESH MUSHROOMS

Store fresh mushrooms in a well-ventilated container, such as an open paper bag, and refrigerate them. Because they're composed of 90 percent water, mushrooms will begin to dehydrate after several days if left at room temperature. Refrigerated in this way, they should last a week or two. When you're ready to use the them, wipe the mushrooms clean with a soft brush or damp cloth.

Both fresh and cooked mushrooms freeze well. To freeze fresh mushrooms, first clean them, and then cut them in half or into ½-inch slices. Spread the slices on a baking sheet, cover, and freeze. Store the frozen mushrooms in airtight containers. Or you can sauté the fresh mushrooms in butter or olive oil until tender, and then freeze them in airtight containers. These will keep up to six months.

ROASTED FALLOW VENISON
Wrapped in Applewood-Smoked Bacon

The Heathman Hotel, Portland, Oregon

Chef Philippe Boulot serves these tender medallions of venison alternating with slices of acorn squash that have been sautéed in butter, brown sugar, and whiskey. Boulot deep-fries the sage leaf garnish that accompanies the venison by simply dropping clean, dry leaves into a small pan of hot oil and removing them when they're lightly browned and fragrant. Balance the earthy intensity of this flavorful dish with a cabernet sauvignon from Washington's Columbia Valley.

1½ pounds venison tenderloin, trimmed of silver skin	¾ pound applewood-smoked bacon or other smoked bacon, thinly sliced
	Sage leaves, for garnish

HUCKLEBERRY GRAND VENEUR SAUCE

½ cup butter	⅓ cup huckleberry jam
½ cup all-purpose flour	1 bottle pinot noir
½ cup minced shallots	⅓ cup huckleberries (fresh or frozen)

PREHEAT THE OVEN to 450°F.

FOR THE SAUCE, first make a roux. In a small saucepan, melt ¼ cup of the butter. Add the flour and cook over low heat for 6 minutes, stirring constantly. Set aside to cool.

WRAP THE VENISON LOIN in bacon, slightly overlapping the slices; the ends do not need to be wrapped. Tie the bacon-wrapped loin with kitchen string, securing it well.

HEAT A HEAVY, OVENPROOF sauté pan or skillet over high heat and sear the venison well on all sides, 4 to 5 minutes in all. Transfer the skillet to the oven and reduce the temperature immediately to 350°F. Roast the venison to the desired doneness, about 12 minutes for medium rare (130°F internal temperature), 15 minutes for medium (140°F).

FINISH THE SAUCE while the venison is roasting. Heat the remaining ¼ cup butter in a large skillet, add the shallots, and cook over medium-high heat until they begin to soften, 1 to 2 minutes. Stir in the huckleberry jam and continue cooking until it begins to bubble and is slightly caramelized, 2 to 3 minutes. Slowly pour in the pinot noir, bring to a boil, and boil until reduced by half, 12 to 15 minutes.

WHEN THE WINE has reduced, stir in the huckleberries. Add the roux, about a tablespoon at a time, stirring well to incorporate each addition, until the sauce has a thick but still pourable consistency. Keep warm over very low heat.

REMOVE THE VENISON roast from the oven, discard the kitchen string, and let the roast sit for a few minutes before carving. To serve, cut the roast into medallions about 1 inch thick. Arrange them around the center of the individual plates, spoon the sauce over them, garnish with sage leaves, and serve immediately.

Makes 4 servings

TO MAKE ROUX

Chef Philippe Boulot, of Portland's Heathman Hotel, offers a good lesson in roux making for his roasted venison recipe:

"Cook the flour and butter over low heat for approximately 6 minutes, stirring constantly and bringing the flour paste off the sides and bottom of the pan. This heated blending period is extremely important. If the temperature is too high, the flour will burn and give off a bitter flavor. If the roux is not cooked long enough, the raw taste will dominate the sauce. Finally, if there is not constant stirring, the flour will not be heated evenly and will not be able to absorb liquid well."

OSSO BUCO OF CARIBOU VENISON

with Garlic-Portobello Ravioli

CinCin, Vancouver, British Columbia

Served with a light, fruity cabernet franc, pinot noir, or chancellor,
hardly anything tastes more satisfying than venison on a chilly winter evening.
If you can't get venison, you can substitute veal shanks.

¼ cup pure olive oil (not extra-virgin)	1 fennel bulb, trimmed, cored, and coarsely
4 caribou shanks (10 to 12 ounces each)	chopped
2 large carrots, coarsely chopped	2 cups bold red wine
1 large onion, coarsely chopped	8 cloves garlic
2 large leeks, white part only, split, cleaned,	1 sprig rosemary
and coarsely chopped	1 sprig thyme
2 large tomatoes, coarsely chopped	1 teaspoon whole black peppercorns
	½ teaspoon ground cinnamon

GARLIC PORTOBELLO RAVIOLI

¾ cup all-purpose flour	1 large portobello mushroom (about 5 ounces),
½ teaspoon salt	cleaned, trimmed, and finely chopped
1 egg	¼ cup minced onion
1 tablespoon olive oil	2 tablespoons minced garlic
	Pinch dried red pepper flakes

PREHEAT THE OVEN to 450°F.

HEAT THE OIL in a large, heavy, ovenproof sauté pan or skillet. Add the caribou shanks
and brown well on all sides. Add the carrots, onion, leeks, tomatoes, fennel, wine, garlic,
rosemary, thyme, peppercorns, and cinnamon. Cover the pan and bake until the meat is
very tender and falling from the bone, about 2 hours.

PREPARE THE RAVIOLI while the venison is baking. Combine the flour and salt in a food processor and pulse just to mix. Add the egg and pulse until the dough forms a ball; if necessary, add a few drops of water. Wrap the pasta dough in plastic and set aside for 30 minutes.

HEAT THE OIL in a large skillet, add the chopped mushroom, onion, and 2 teaspoons of the garlic and sauté until the mushroom is tender and its liquid has evaporated, 4 to 5 minutes. Stir in the red pepper flakes. Taste the mixture for seasoning, adding salt to taste.

ROLL THE PASTA DOUGH in a pasta machine to a thickness of ⅛ inch (the next-to-last setting on the rollers) and lay the sheet on the work surface. Brush half of the dough lightly with water and sprinkle the moistened half with the remaining 4 teaspoons minced garlic. Spoon the mushroom filling onto the moistened half of the dough in 4 mounds at least 2 inches apart. Fold the other half of the dough over, carefully pressing down so the filling is fully sealed inside the dough. Cut the over-sized ravioli apart with a ravioli wheel or sharp knife. Set aside on a lightly floured tray. Cover with a towel and let sit.

WHEN THE CARIBOU SHANKS are done, bring a large pot of lightly salted water to a boil. Add the ravioli and simmer until al dente, about 5 minutes. Drain well and place 1 ravioli on each individual plate. Top each with a caribou shank and some of the vegetables, spooning some of the cooking liquid over all. (If the liquid is very thin, you can boil it to reduce it slightly.) Serve immediately.

Makes 4 servings

VENISON

Many people consider venison the meat of the '90s because it contains only 3 to 5 percent fat (compared to beef at 20 percent fat) and almost no cholesterol. Some of the freshest, mildest-tasting venison comes from fallow deer, which have been raised in captivity for more than 5,000 years. Fallow deer is currently raised on a small scale throughout the Northwest, and the meat is available at specialty butcher shops.

Besides being milder in flavor than wild venison, farm-raised fallow deer are much more tender. Recipes for wild venison often call for acidic marinades and a long, slow cooking process to tame the wild flavor and tenderize the meat. With farm-raised fallow deer, these steps are unnecessary. Cuts can be treated much like good-quality cuts of lean beef.

MINUTE VENISON

Holiday Farm, Blue River, Oregon

At the Holiday Farm, on the McKenzie River, this amazingly
quick dish is served with mixed sautéed vegetables and a baked stuffed potato.
To complement the rich, earthy flavors of venison, pour a hearty
Chateau Ste. Michelle cabernet sauvignon.

1½ pounds venison filet
2 tablespoons butter
¼ cup minced flat-leaf (Italian) parsley

¼ cup minced green onion tops
Salt and freshly ground black pepper

CUT THE VENISON into ¼-inch slices, using a very sharp knife. Heat the butter in
a large skillet over medium heat, add the parsley and green onion, and cook until just
tender, 1 to 2 minutes. Add the venison slices, season with salt and pepper, and cook
over medium-high heat for 1 minute. You may need to cook the venison in batches.
Turn the venison and continue cooking until done to taste, 2 to 3 minutes longer.
Arrange the venison on a serving platter or individual plates. Spoon the parsley, green
onion, and cooking juices over it and serve immediately.

Makes 4 servings

BASIC BEEF OR VEAL STOCK

Ask your butcher to cut large bones into smaller pieces; they shouldn't weigh much over 1 pound each. Because stocks are often reduced to concentrate the flavor in recipes, it is best not to use salt when making stock. Season as needed when the stock is added to the recipe.

For a light-colored stock, simply simmer (don't roast) the bones and vegetables. For a richer-flavored stock, boil the strained stock until reduced by about one-quarter.

4 pounds beef or veal bones
2 onions, quartered
2 large carrots, coarsely chopped
2 stalks celery, coarsely chopped

Bouquet garni of 3 parsley stems,
2 sprigs thyme, and 1 bay leaf, tied
*   together with string*
1 teaspoon black peppercorns
12 cups water (more if needed)

PREHEAT THE OVEN to 425°F.

PUT THE BONES in a large roasting pan and scatter the onions, carrots, and celery around them. Roast until the bones are well browned, about 30 minutes. Stir occasionally so the bones brown evenly.

TRANSFER THE BONES and vegetables to a stockpot; add the bouquet garni and peppercorns. Add cold water to cover, bring to a boil, then lower the heat and simmer, uncovered, until the stock is brown and richly flavored, 3 to 4 hours. If necessary, add more hot water to the pot as it simmers so that the bones are always covered. Use a large spoon to skim off scum that rises to the top.

LIFT THE BONES from the stock with tongs and discard them. Strain the stock through a fine sieve or a colander lined with cheesecloth, discarding the solids. Let cool, then skim off fat that rises to the surface. Chill and use within a few days, or freeze for up to 1 month.

Makes about 8 cups

CARETTO D'AGNELLO

Il Bistro, Seattle, Washington

Rich and and robustly flavored, this delicious rack of lamb is worthy of a special Northwest red wine, such as a big, powerful D2 from Washington's DeLille Cellars. Note that the rack of lamb needs to marinate for one to two days.

1 rack of lamb, trimmed (about 8 ribs, 1½ pounds total)

MARINADE

¼ cup chopped garlic	*1 tablespoon sea salt or other salt*
2 tablespoons chopped rosemary	*2 large lemons, halved*
2 tablespoons chopped oregano	*1½ cups olive oil*

RED WINE SAUCE

1 tablespoon red wine vinegar	*Pinch chopped rosemary*
2 cups red wine	*Pinch chopped garlic*
1 cup beef or veal stock (see page 139)	*2 tablespoons butter*
½ cup stewed or chopped fresh tomatoes	*Salt and freshly ground black pepper*

FOR THE MARINADE, combine the garlic, rosemary, oregano, salt, lemon halves (lightly squeezed to release a little juice), and olive oil in a shallow pan. Add the lamb and rub all over with the marinade. Cover and let marinate in the refrigerator for 1 to 2 days, turning the rack a few times.

PREHEAT THE OVEN to 450°F.

HEAT A LARGE SAUTÉ PAN or skillet over medium-high heat. Remove the lamb from the marinade, put it in the pan, and brown it quickly on all sides. Transfer to a roasting pan and bake for 10 to 15 minutes for medium rare.

PREPARE THE SAUCE while the lamb is roasting. Discard all but 1 tablespoon of drippings from the sauté pan and reheat the pan. Add the vinegar and stir to deglaze the pan. Add the wine, stock, tomatoes, rosemary, and garlic, bring to a boil, and boil until reduced to about ¾ cup. Remove the pan from the heat, add the butter, and stir to gently melt it into the sauce. Season to taste with salt and pepper.

REMOVE THE LAMB from the oven and let it sit for a few minutes. Carve the rack into chops and serve with the sauce.

Makes 2 servings

ORANGE-SPICED LAMB SHANKS

Raku Kushiyaki, Vancouver, British Columbia

Hardly any food is more comforting on a cold fall or winter evening than meltingly tender lamb shanks, the meat falling off the bone. First simmered in a fragrant broth and then browned outdoors on a grill or inside under a broiler, these shanks blend nicely with a full-bodied cabernet-merlot from Snoqualmie Winery.

2 oranges	*3 cloves garlic*
8 cups chicken stock (see page 81)	*1 cinnamon stick*
or beef stock (see page 139)	*1 tablespoon Sichuan peppercorns*
1 cup soy sauce	*2 dried black mushrooms (optional)*
¾ cup packed brown sugar	*6 lamb shanks (about 1 pound each)*
¾ cup sake or dry sherry	

GINGER AIOLI

2 egg yolks	*Juice of 1 lemon*
1 teaspoon white wine vinegar	*2 tablespoons minced or grated ginger*
1 teaspoon Dijon-style mustard	*½ cup loosely packed flat-leaf*
1 cup garlic oil, or 1 cup vegetable oil	*(Italian) parsley*
and 1 clove garlic	*Salt and freshly ground black pepper*

PEEL STRIPS OF ZEST from the oranges, using a vegetable peeler, and then squeeze the juice.

STIR TOGETHER THE STOCK, soy sauce, brown sugar, sake, garlic, cinnamon, peppercorns, mushrooms, orange zest, and orange juice in a large, heavy pot. Add the lamb shanks and bring the mixture just to a boil. Reduce the heat, cover the pot, and simmer until the lamb is very tender, about 3 hours. Let the meat cool in the cooking liquid, then remove the shanks and refrigerate until needed.

PREPARE THE AIOLI while the lamb simmers. Combine the egg yolks, vinegar, and mustard in a food processor. With the motor running, add the oil through the tube, drizzling it very slowly at first. Once the mixture begins to emulsify, continue adding the oil in a steady stream. Add the lemon juice, ginger, garlic (if using vegetable oil instead of garlic oil), and parsley and continue processing until the parsley is very finely chopped and the aioli is an even green color. Season to taste with salt and pepper and chill until ready to serve.

LIGHT AN OUTDOOR GRILL or preheat the broiler. Grill or broil the lamb shanks, turning so they become evenly crisp, 4 to 5 minutes in all. Arrange the shanks on a platter and pass the ginger aioli separately.

Makes 6 servings

ROSEMARY LAMB
with Curry Yogurt Sauce

Chef Bernard's Inn and Restaurant, Kimberley, British Columbia

These tender lamb chops are best cooked over an outdoor grill, but you could also bake them in the oven at 400°F for 8 to 10 minutes. Garlic black bean sauce can be used in place of sweet black bean sauce. Match this robust dish with an intensely flavored Erath Vintage Select Pinot Noir from Oregon's Willamette Valley.

1 cup unsweetened coconut milk
2 tablespoons dried rosemary, finely crushed
2 tablespoons chopped garlic
1 tablespoon Thai fish sauce (nam pla)
1 tablespoon Thai sweet black bean sauce or other black bean sauce
1 tablespoon curry powder
2 teaspoons ground white pepper

2 teaspoons ground black pepper
1 teaspoon minced jalapeño or serrano chile
12 lamb chops, ¾ inch thick (about 2½ pounds)
2 tablespoons olive oil
1 cup plain lowfat yogurt
Rosemary sprigs, for garnish

COMBINE THE COCONUT MILK, rosemary, garlic, fish sauce, black bean sauce, curry powder, white and black peppers, and chile in a large bowl. Add the lamb chops and turn to coat them evenly. Cover the bowl and refrigerate for 6 hours or overnight.

REMOVE THE LAMB CHOPS from the marinade and set aside. Heat the olive oil in a small skillet, add the marinade, and cook over medium heat, stirring constantly, for 3 minutes. Strain the marinade through a fine sieve and stir 1 tablespoon of it into the yogurt. Discard the remaining marinade.

LIGHT AN OUTDOOR GRILL. When hot, put the lamb chops on the grate and grill until they reach the desired doneness, about 3 minutes per side for medium rare, 4 minutes for medium.

ARRANGE 3 CHOPS on each plate, spoon the yogurt sauce alongside them, and garnish with sprigs of rosemary. Serve immediately.

Makes 4 servings

NORTHWEST LAMB

No matter where lamb is raised in the pristine farmlands of the Pacific Northwest, whether on Saltspring Island, British Columbia, or in Ellensburg, Washington, its exceptionally mild, sweet flavor blends wonderfully with woodsy mushrooms, earthy root vegetables, toasted nuts, fruity olive oil, and savory herbs like garlic and rosemary.

To be designated as lamb, meat must come from an animal that is less than one year old. Once a seasonal item, lamb is now available year-round, in the form of leg of lamb, chops, racks, the sirloin leg steak (great for grilling), and top round roast (which can be sliced into medallions or steaks or roasted whole). Thanks to new standards in the lamb industry, instituted in 1990, consumers are assured of mild-flavored, lean, tender meat.

Judge freshness in lamb by the firmness of the legs, which should be thick and plump. Fat should be firm and white or creamy in color. Flesh should be firm, fine grained, and smooth and velvety to the touch. Meat should be light pink in color, and should smell sweet and herbaceous.

GINGERED PORK TENDERLOIN
with Wok-Seared Chinese Greens

Beach Side Cafe, West Vancouver, British Columbia

Seasoned with honey and fresh ginger, this pork loin is served with a tangy
tamarind shallot sauce and a mix of sautéed Chinese greens. If you are unable
to find Chinese broccoli greens, use chopped broccoli in its place. Tamarind is a
highly astringent beanlike pod often used in Asian cookery. It can be purchased
in blocks of pulp, in paste, or as concentrate. If using concentrate, use
half of the amount called for in this recipe.

2 pounds pork tenderloin,	*1 tablespoon honey*
preferably 2 to 3 small loins	*2 tablespoons vegetable oil*
1 tablespoon grated ginger	

TAMARIND SHALLOT SAUCE

1 tablespoon sesame oil	*1 cup chicken stock*
1 shallot, thinly sliced	*½ cup white wine*
½ teaspoon minced garlic	*2 teaspoons tamarind pulp,*
½ teaspoon grated ginger	*or 1 teaspoon concentrate*

WOK-SEARED CHINESE GREENS

2 teaspoons sesame oil	*1 teaspoon grated ginger*
2 teaspoons vegetable oil	*1 teaspoon minced garlic*
2 baby bok choy, halved	*2 teaspoons white wine*
½ pound Chinese broccoli greens (gai lan),	*1 teaspoon soy sauce*
tough ends trimmed and stalks halved	

WITH A SHARP KNIFE, trim away any white sinew and excess fat from the pork tenderloins. Thoroughly rub the meat with the ginger and honey. Set aside at room temperature for 20 minutes.

PREHEAT THE OVEN to 400°F.

HEAT THE OIL in a large, heavy skillet over medium-high heat. Add the pork loins and sear them on all sides. Transfer the loins to a roasting pan and roast until just a hint of pink remains at the center (a meat thermometer should register 160°F), 20 to 30 minutes.

PREPARE THE SAUCE while the pork is roasting. Heat the 1 tablespoon of sesame oil in the pan that the pork was seared in. Add the shallot, garlic, and ginger and sauté until fragrant, 1 to 2 minutes. Add the chicken stock and white wine and stir to dissolve tasty bits stuck to the pan. Add the tamarind pulp, bring to a boil, and boil until reduced by about half. Season to taste with salt and pepper. Keep warm.

FOR THE SEARED GREENS, heat a wok over high heat. Add the 2 teaspoons of sesame oil and the vegetable oil and heat until just smoking. Add the bok choy, broccoli greens, and ginger and stir-fry for 1 minute. Add the garlic and continue stir-frying 1 minute longer. Stir in the white wine and soy sauce, cover the wok, and cook until the vegetables are just crisp-tender, 2 to 3 minutes longer.

WHEN THE PORK is done, transfer the tenderloins to a carving board and let sit for a few minutes. Slice the tenderloins into 1-inch-thick medallions. Place the greens in the center of individual plates and arrange the medallions around them. Drizzle the sauce over the roasted pork; serve immediately.

Makes 4 servings

CRANBERRY POT ROAST

Tokeland Hotel & Restaurant, Tokeland, Washington

Some of the Northwest's most prized cranberry bogs are just a skipping-stone's-throw away from the Tokeland Hotel near Willapa Bay, so this variation on pot roast is a natural. When fresh berries aren't available, look for frozen or dried cranberries, or use 1 cup canned whole berries. Mashed potatoes and a fresh, fruity pinot noir from Montinore Vineyards complete this meal.

1 cup all-purpose flour	1 cup dry white wine or water
1 teaspoon salt	1 stick cinnamon, broken into 2 or 3 pieces
½ teaspoon freshly ground black pepper	10 whole cloves
1 rump or bottom round beef roast,	2 cups whole cranberries
5 to 6 pounds	1 cup water
Vegetable oil	½ cup sugar

GRAVY

¼ cup cornstarch	2 cups beef stock (see page 139)
½ cup dry red wine	Salt and freshly ground black pepper

PREHEAT THE OVEN to 350°F.

COMBINE THE FLOUR, salt, and pepper and thoroughly coat the roast in the seasoned flour. Over medium-high heat, heat about ¼ inch of oil in the bottom of a heavy Dutch oven or other heavy pan large enough to hold the roast. Add the roast and brown well on all sides. Add the wine, cinnamon stick, and cloves. Cover the pan and roast in the oven until the meat is quite tender, 3 to 3½ hours.

COOK THE CRANBERRIES while the meat is roasting. In a small pan, combine the cranberries, water, and sugar and simmer, stirring often, just until the sugar has dissolved and the berries begin to burst. Set aside.

WHEN THE ROAST IS TENDER, remove the pan from the oven and carefully ladle out and reserve all but about ½ inch of the pan drippings. Pour the cranberries and their liquid over the roast and return it to the oven, uncovered, for about 30 minutes.

MAKE THE GRAVY while the roast is finishing. Put the reserved pan drippings in a small saucepan. In a small bowl, stir together the cornstarch and wine. Add this mixture and the beef stock to the saucepan. Cook over medium heat, stirring constantly, just until the sauce thickens. Season to taste with salt and pepper.

TRANSFER THE ROAST to a carving board and cut into thick slices. Arrange the slices on a serving platter and spoon the cranberries and remaining pan drippings over. Serve immediately, passing the gravy separately.

Makes 8 to 10 servings

BAKED CHILEAN SEA BASS
in Black Bean Sauce

Delilah's, Vancouver, British Columbia

Sea bass is a delicate-flavored, firm-fleshed white fish. You can also use salmon, halibut, or flounder in this versatile recipe. Round out the meal with blanched asparagus and grilled red and yellow peppers.

1 to 2 tablespoons vegetable oil | *1½ pounds Chilean sea bass fillet,*
cut into 4 portions

BLACK BEAN SAUCE

½ cup freshly squeezed orange juice | *1½ teaspoons freshly squeezed lime juice*
¼ cup dry sherry | *1½ teaspoons minced cilantro*
¼ cup sake | *½ teaspoon minced garlic*
¼ cup oyster sauce | *½ teaspoon minced ginger*
3½ tablespoons fermented | *½ teaspoon minced jalapeño*
black beans, chopped | *½ teaspoon cornstarch*
2 tablespoons soy sauce |

FOR THE BLACK BEAN SAUCE, combine the orange juice, sherry, sake, oyster sauce, black beans, soy sauce, lime juice, cilantro, garlic, ginger, jalapeño, and cornstarch in a medium bowl and whisk to mix well. Set aside.

PREHEAT THE OVEN to 350°F.

HEAT THE OIL in a large, ovenproof skillet over medium-high heat. Add the fish and cook until well browned, about 1 minute per side. Remove the skillet from the heat, pour the black bean sauce over the fish, and put the pan in the oven to bake until the fish is just cooked through, 8 to 10 minutes longer.

SET A PORTION of the fish onto each of 4 individual plates. If the black bean sauce has not thickened, boil until reduced slightly. Spoon the black bean sauce over and around the fish and serve.

Makes 4 servings

BUYING FISH 101

Selecting quality fish is no more difficult than choosing good-quality fruits or vegetables. It's simply a matter of using your senses. Look for fish that smell clean and invigorating. The scales should be intact, and the bright, iridescent skin protected by a slippery, viscous coating. The body should be firm and elastic, bouncing back when you press it, and the eyes bright, round, and transparent.

It also helps to know how the fish was harvested, cleaned, and transported. Fish caught in gill nets are more likely to have bruised, spotted flesh than fish caught with a hook and line. Further bruising can occur while the fish are stored in the boat holds. Also, fish should be bled and gutted immediately after capture. Some fishers flash-freeze the fish aboard ship after cleaning them.

When buying a whole fish, check inside of it to make sure it's been properly cleaned. Look for bright-red gills. Avoid fish with "belly burns" (brown spots of deterioration), dark spots in the flesh, loss of scales, a fishy smell, or tears in the skin.

When buying fish fillets and steaks, look for shiny, translucent flesh with no fishy odor. Avoid any white fish that has pink bruise spots or that is gray or brown (which indicates aging). With fish that have tan or cream-colored flesh, such as tuna or shark, avoid any that have dark (blood) streaks.

If a fish is not chilled properly, the quality will deteriorate rapidly. Whole fish should be buried in ice, which will keep the temperature of the fish at 32°F. As the ice melts, it rinses away bacteria. Fillets should be wrapped and kept chilled at 32°F *over* ice; ice sitting on top of a fillet will seep into it. Freezing fish at home is not recommended. Most home freezers do not maintain cold enough temperatures to prevent ice crystals from damaging the fish.

ROASTED RED KING SALMON
with Pesto Crust and Spinach and Tomato Napoleons

The Heathman Hotel, Portland, Oregon

For a special occasion, try this fragrant pesto-encrusted king
salmon, served with a flavorful napoleon made with layers of oven-dried beefsteak
tomatoes and fresh spinach. Note that the tomatoes need to dry in the oven for at
least 2 hours, so plan ahead; they can be prepared one day in advance and
stored in an airtight container.

4 salmon fillet pieces (7 to 8 ounces each), pin bones removed

SPINACH AND TOMATO NAPOLEONS

½ teaspoon ground coriander
½ teaspoon ground cumin
½ teaspoon freshly ground black pepper
½ teaspoon salt
½ teaspoon minced garlic

*2 large, ripe beefsteak tomatoes, cored and cut
in ¼-inch slices*
¼ cup olive oil
1 shallot, minced
*1½ pounds spinach, tough stems removed
(about 2 bunches)*

PESTO CRUST

¼ cup coarsely chopped basil
¼ cup bread crumbs
2 tablespoons pine nuts
2 tablespoons grated Parmesan cheese

2 slices bacon, chopped
1 clove garlic
2 tablespoons olive oil

RED ONION CILANTRO RELISH

2 tablespoons olive oil
*1 large or 2 small red onions, diced
(about 2 cups)*
½ teaspoon minced garlic
½ teaspoon minced ginger
¼ cup freshly squeezed lemon juice
1 tablespoon soy sauce

*1 teaspoon red chile garlic paste (such as
sambal oelek) or minced fresh chile*
1 teaspoon drained capers
1 teaspoon thinly sliced green onion
1 teaspoon minced flat-leaf (Italian) parsley
1 teaspoon minced cilantro

PREHEAT THE OVEN to 200°F.

TO OVEN-DRY THE TOMATOES, stir together the coriander, cumin, pepper, salt, and garlic in a small bowl. Line a baking sheet with parchment paper or foil and sprinkle half of the seasonings over it. Arrange the tomato slices on the sheet, brush the tops with 2 tablespoons of the olive oil, and sprinkle the remaining seasonings over them. Dry in the oven until slightly wrinkled looking, 2 to 3 hours. Set aside on paper towels.

HEAT THE REMAINING 2 tablespoons olive oil in a large skillet, add the shallot, and sauté for 1 minute. Add the spinach and cook, stirring, until thoroughly wilted. Season to taste with salt and pepper and set aside.

FOR THE PESTO CRUST, combine the basil, bread crumbs, pine nuts, Parmesan cheese, bacon, and garlic in a food processor and process until well mixed. With the machine running, slowly add the olive oil. Season to taste with salt and pepper.

FOR THE RELISH, heat the olive oil in a large skillet over medium-high heat. Add the red onion and cook, stirring, until the onion gives off some liquid and begins to soften, 3 to 4 minutes. Add the garlic and ginger and cook for 1 minute longer. Stir in the lemon juice and continue cooking until most of the liquid has evaporated, about 2 minutes. Stir in the soy sauce, chile garlic paste, capers, green onion, parsley, and cilantro. Taste the mixture for seasoning, transfer to a bowl, and refrigerate. (Cooling the relish quickly helps preserve the texture and color of the onions.)

PREHEAT THE OVEN to 400°F.

PRESS THE PESTO CRUST mixture onto the flesh side of each salmon fillet piece, forming a crust about ⅛ inch thick. Heat a large, ovenproof, nonstick skillet until very hot, add the salmon, crust side down, and sear until nicely browned, 1 to 2 minutes. Flip the salmon crust side up, put it in the oven and bake until just opaque in the center, about 5 to 8 minutes, depending on the thickness of the fillets.

ASSEMBLE THE SPINACH and tomato napoleons while the salmon is baking. On each of 4 plates, press 1 tablespoon of the spinach mixture into a small circle and set a tomato slice on top. Add another layer of spinach, and top with another tomato slice. Repeat once more, for a triple-layer napoleon.

SPOON SOME RED ONION relish onto each plate and set the pesto-crusted salmon on top. Serve immediately, passing any remaining relish separately.

Makes 4 servings

SALMON PICCATA STYLE

Roberto's Restaurant, Friday Harbor, Washington

Faced with only four burners in his restaurant—no oven or grill—chef Roberto Carrieri asked himself what an Italian chef might do with a piece of salmon and a sauté pan. The answer took inspiration from the classic veal piccata, marrying salmon with lemon, capers, and butter. With this lively salmon dish, serve a rich, opulent pinot gris or chardonnay, such as the King Estate Reserve Oregon Pinot Gris.

1½ pounds salmon fillet, preferably a thick piece, skin and pin bones removed

3 to 4 tablespoons clarified butter or olive oil

¼ cup all-purpose flour (more if needed)

¾ cup dry white wine

Juice of 1 lemon, or to taste

½ cup unsalted butter, cut in pieces and chilled

¼ cup drained capers

Salt and freshly ground black pepper

Lemon wedges, for serving

SLICE THE SALMON CROSSWISE into pieces about ½ inch thick, using a very sharp knife.

HEAT THE CLARIFIED BUTTER in a sauté pan or large skillet. While the butter is heating, coat each salmon piece with flour, patting to remove the excess. When the butter is hot, add the salmon slices and cook until lightly browned and just cooked through, about 2 minutes on each side. Transfer the salmon to a plate and set aside.

POUR OFF AND DISCARD the excess butter from the pan. Add the wine and lemon juice to the pan and bring just to a boil, stirring to dissolve the flavorful bits stuck to the pan. Boil for 1 to 2 minutes to reduce the liquid slightly. Lower the heat and add the chilled butter and capers, with salt and pepper to taste, gently swirling the pan to melt the butter. Just before the butter is fully incorporated, return the salmon to the pan and continue swirling to coat the salmon in sauce. Divide the salmon among 4 individual warmed plates, spoon the sauce over it, and serve, with lemon wedges on the side for squeezing over the salmon.

Makes 4 servings

King, chinook, tyee, or blackmouth: This is the largest and rarest of the Pacific species, averaging 15 to 40 pounds, with some specimens weighing up to 100 pounds. Kings, whose flesh color ranges from a rich "salmon" shade to almost white, are highly prized for their fat content, which imparts complex flavor and rich texture. Kings are mainly available from May to September. The fattest king salmon are Columbia River chinooks, Alaskan Yukon kings, and Copper River kings.

Coho, or silver: Average market size for the coho salmon is 5 to 10 pounds, although some can grow to over 20 pounds. Like the meat of a king salmon, coho meat, which ranges in color from rich orange-red to pale pink, forms large flakes when cooked. Cohos are firm fleshed and extremely flavorful. Their season runs from July through September.

Sockeye, red, or blueback: The deep-red flesh of sockeye is tightly grained, with a robust flavor. These are the second fattiest of the Pacific salmon, generally weighing 5 to 7 pounds. They are available from late May through July. Look for fish from British Columbia's Fraser River and Alaska's Cooper River.

Chum, keta, dog, or fall: Chum meat is less fatty than other salmon and usually paler in color; some chums, however, have a good reddish-orange color and earthy flavor. These fish are available from July through October.

Pink, or humpie: Pinks are the smallest and most abundant of the Pacific salmon. The meat, as the name suggests, is usually pink in color and delicately flavored. Because of their small size, pinks are excellent for grilling whole; however, most of the pink harvest goes into cans.

HERBED BAKED SALMON
on Rock Salt with Late-Summer Tomato Salad

Wildwood, Portland, Oregon

Slow-baking salmon on a bed of rock salt helps distribute heat more evenly, ensuring moist texture and rich flavor. For a festive tomato salad, use yellow and red pear tomatoes, cherry tomatoes, and currant tomatoes.

1½ pounds salmon fillet, skin on, pin bones removed	*1 tablespoon minced flat-leaf (Italian) parsley*
1 tablespoon minced tarragon	*1 tablespoon minced thyme*
1 tablespoon minced basil	*1 tablespoon fennel seeds, lightly crushed*
	3 cups rock salt or kosher salt (more if needed)

TOMATO SALAD

1 pound mixed tomatoes, halved	*½ cup olive oil*
½ red onion, halved and sliced	*2 tablespoons balsamic vinegar*
3 cloves garlic, minced	*Salt and freshly ground black pepper*
½ bunch basil, rinsed, stems removed (about ½ cup lightly packed leaves)	

PREHEAT THE OVEN to 325°F.

RUB THE SALMON with the minced herbs and fennel seeds, distributing them evenly. Season lightly with salt and pepper. Cover a large baking sheet with foil and spread the rock salt over it.

SET THE SALMON FILLET, skin side down, on the bed of salt and bake it until the fish is just cooked through, 35 to 45 minutes.

PREPARE THE TOMATO SALAD while the salmon bakes. Combine the tomatoes, onion, garlic, and basil in a large bowl. Drizzle the olive oil and vinegar over the salad, toss gently to mix, and season to taste with salt and pepper. Let sit for at least 15 minutes before serving.

WHEN THE SALMON is done, remove the pan from the oven and let sit for 5 minutes. Brush off excess salt, cut the fillet into 4 serving portions, and arrange on individual plates. Spoon the tomato salad alongside the salmon and serve.

Makes 4 servings

SALMON IN THE NATIVE TRADITION

Salmon played a central role in the lives and cultures of Northwest Native Americans. Many tribes believed that they and the salmon were descended from the same ancestors, and that salmon sacrificed themselves to benefit humankind. When a Chinook fisherman caught the season's first salmon, the fish was eaten ceremonially, and the heart was removed and thrown back to the sea to ensure new life.

The Native peoples still hold salmon celebrations each spring to honor the first salmon of the season. One of the oldest and largest salmon celebrations in the Northwest is the Celilo Wy-Am Salmon Feast and Pow Wow, held each April at the Celilo Village, just east of The Dalles on the Oregon side of the Columbia River. Before The Dalles Dam was built in 1957, Celilo Falls, one of the largest falls on the Columbia River, was a mecca for Indian fishermen, who gathered by the thousands each spring and fall to spear or net salmon.

In the traditional Native method of cooking salmon, the fish is held in a sturdy split pole with an interlacing web of cedar sticks. The pole is stuck in the ground near a slow-burning fire, one with glowing embers that emit a steady heat. (Northwest alder is the favored wood for cooking salmon.) The salmon cooks slowly, basting itself with its own oils while absorbing the fragrant smoke of the fire. Salmon cooked this way achieves a complexity of flavors and textures unattainable with any other method.

SALMON BAKE

Jot's Resort, Gold Beach, Oregon

It's no surprise that magnificent Rogue River salmon are a specialty
at this Oregon fishing resort, located on the north bank of the Rogue River.
This salmon bake may become a specialty at your house too.

¼ cup butter, melted
3 tablespoons Dijon-style mustard
1½ tablespoons honey
¼ cup bread crumbs
¼ cup very finely chopped pecans

4 teaspoons minced flat-leaf (Italian) parsley
4 salmon fillet pieces (about 6 ounces each)
Salt and freshly ground black pepper
Lemon wedges, for serving

PREHEAT THE OVEN to 450°F.

STIR TOGETHER the butter, mustard, and honey in a small bowl and set aside. In
another bowl, stir together the bread crumbs, pecans, and parsley.

LIGHTLY SEASON the salmon with salt and pepper and set the pieces on a lightly
greased baking sheet. Brush the salmon generously with the mustard–honey mixture and
sprinkle the bread crumb mixture over it. Bake the salmon until just cooked through, 10
to 15 minutes, depending on the thickness of the fillets. Transfer the salmon to individual
plates, with a lemon wedge alongside for squeezing over the fish. Serve immediately.

Makes 4 servings

FLASH-FREEZING: WHEN FROZEN MEANS FRESH

Bruce Gore has been fishing the waters of Southeast Alaska for more than 25 years. During that time, he has developed a unique process of flash freezing just-caught salmon aboard ship. Gore's flash-freezing process has not only given him an edge on the competition—it also has greatly influenced the quality of salmon available on the Northwest market.

"Most fish is frozen by default, because it's too old," explains Gore. "What we do is designate fish to be frozen from the beginning, when it's in its prime. Fish that is nonfrozen is often mistakenly labeled as 'fresh.' But the opposite of fresh is not frozen—it's rotten."

The flash-freezing process starts aboard the fishing boat, where the salmon are caught with hook and line. Each fish is pulled to the side of the boat and stunned with a gaff hook, leaving the fish intact. Once the fish are aboard, they are live-bled, eviscerated, and flash frozen at -40°F, all within a matter of minutes.

Gore refers to this process as "stopping the biological clock." "The fish are frozen pre-rigor mortis," he explains, "so there is no enzymatic activity to degrade the product." Gore has each fish marked with a colored tag bearing his name and a number, enabling him to track when and where each fish was caught.

When Gore's salmon are thawed, they are so clean and brilliant, you'd swear they had just been pulled from the icy waters. Culinary luminaries, including Julia Child (who featured a Bruce Gore king salmon on one of her cooking shows), have selected Gore's frozen fish over nonfrozen in blind taste tests. In Japan, where his salmon are favored for sashimi, Gore's fish set the quality standard against which they judge all other salmon.

TWO FISH IN PHYLLO

Gourmet by the Sea, Campbell River, British Columbia

Chef Michel Rabu created this dish in response to his guests' requests for a seafood dish that was "light, crisp, and fresh." Salmon and halibut fillets are wrapped in packets of buttery phyllo dough and topped with a tropical guava and pineapple sauce. Knorr brand packaged béarnaise sauce can be substituted for homemade béarnaise with good results.

¾ pound salmon fillet, skin and pin bones removed	*¼ cup butter, melted*
¾ pound halibut fillet, skin and pin bones removed	*8 large sorrel or spinach leaves, rinsed and dried*
4 sheets phyllo dough	*4 teaspoons prepared béarnaise sauce*

GUAVA SAUCE

¾ cup guava nectar	*1 tablespoon arrowroot or cornstarch,*
¾ cup pineapple juice	*dissolved in 2 tablespoons water*
1 teaspoon curry powder	

PREHEAT THE OVEN to 375°F.

CUT THE SALMON and halibut fillets into 4 equal pieces (for a total of 8 pieces), preferably all the same size (about 1 inch by 4 inches).

LAY ONE PHYLLO sheet on the work surface, with the long side toward you. (Keep the remaining phyllo covered with a towel so it doesn't dry out.) Brush the sheet with some of the melted butter and fold it in half crosswise. Set one of the sorrel leaves about 2 inches from the bottom. Set one piece of salmon and one piece of halibut side by side on top. Spread 1 teaspoon of the béarnaise sauce over the fish and top with another sorrel leaf. Fold the bottom 2 inches of the phyllo over the filling, then fold the sides in towards the center. Roll the phyllo up, fully enclosing the fish. Brush the outside of the roll lightly with butter and set it seam side down on a baking sheet. Repeat with the remaining phyllo and filling ingredients.

BAKE THE PHYLLO rolls until golden brown, 12 to 15 minutes.

MAKE THE SAUCE while the rolls are cooking. Combine the guava nectar and pine-apple juice in a small saucepan and bring to a boil. Stir in the curry powder and simmer for about 2 minutes. Stir in the dissolved arrowroot and continue simmering until thick-ened, about 2 minutes longer. Set aside and keep warm until ready to serve.

SET A PHYLLO ROLL on each of 4 individual plates, drizzle with guava sauce, and serve immediately.

Makes 4 servings

STEELHEAD

Wild West Coast steelhead, or saltwater rainbow trout, are anadro-mous, meaning that they live in saltwater but spawn in freshwater rivers (like most salmon species). The flesh color ranges from ivory to brilliant red, depending on the fish's diet. Fish that consume large quantities of crayfish or shrimp will be more vibrantly colored. Steelhead meat is gen-erally dark pink when cooked, similar to salmon, and is very flavorful.

Wild steelhead are usually larger than inland rainbow trout, and fish weighing 6 to 12 pounds are not uncommon. In the Northwest there are two wild steelhead runs, one during the summer months and the other in the winter, from December through April. Because just a tiny commercial harvest of wild steelhead is allowed in the Pacific Northwest, these fish can be difficult to find. It is illegal to sell wild steelhead in Oregon, but they can be caught there and sold outside the state. In Washington, Native American fishermen can catch and sell wild steelhead on a highly regulated basis.

ROASTED STEELHEAD
with Mint-Hazelnut Pesto

River Place Hotel, Portland, Oregon

This is comfort food, ideal for those wet, wintry days for which the Northwest is famous. The recipe combines three favorite Northwest ingredients— steelhead, hazelnuts, and mint.

2¼ pounds steelhead fillet, cut into 6 serving pieces | 1 tablespoon vegetable oil

MINT-HAZELNUT PESTO

1 cup loosely packed spearmint leaves
5 cloves garlic
¼ cup pine nuts
¼ cup grated Parmesan cheese

½ cup olive oil
Salt and freshly ground black pepper
½ cup hazelnuts, toasted and coarsely chopped

FRESH TOMATO COULIS

6 plum (Roma) tomatoes (about 1 pound), cored and quartered

2 tablespoons extra-virgin olive oil

MASHED POTATOES WITH CELERY ROOT AND PEAR

1 pound russet potatoes, peeled and cut in 1-inch dice
1 pound celery root, peeled and cut in 1-inch dice

1 pound pears, preferably Bartlett or d'Anjou, peeled and cut in 1-inch dice
½ cup milk
2 tablespoons butter

FOR THE PESTO, combine the mint, garlic, pine nuts, and Parmesan cheese in a food processor and blend until very smooth. With the machine running, slowly pour in the olive oil. Season to taste with salt and pepper. Transfer the pesto to a bowl and stir in the chopped hazelnuts. Set aside.

FOR THE TOMATO COULIS, purée the tomatoes in a food processor or blender. Add the olive oil and continue processing until the coulis is thick and well mixed. Pass the mixture through a strainer to remove seeds and bits of skin. Season to taste with salt and pepper, put the coulis in a small saucepan, and gently warm over low heat.

FOR THE MASHED POTATOES, combine the potato and celery root in a large pan with just enough water to cover. Bring to a boil, lower the heat, and simmer until the potatoes are nearly tender, 12 to 15 minutes. Add the pears and simmer 5 minutes longer. Meanwhile, heat the milk with the butter in a small saucepan just until the butter has melted. Drain the potato mixture well and return it to the pan. Add the warm milk mixture and mash. (Do not thoroughly purée the mixture—a few lumps are desirable.) Season to taste with salt and pepper and cover the pan to keep warm.

PREHEAT THE OVEN to 375°F.

DRIZZLE THE STEELHEAD pieces with the oil and rub it thoroughly over the fish. Heat a large, ovenproof skillet, preferably nonstick, over high heat. Add the fish pieces, skin side up, and sear for 1 to 2 minutes. (Don't disturb the fish for the first minute or it will stick.) Turn the fish and sear on the skin side for 1 to 2 minutes. Spread about 1 tablespoon of the pesto over each piece of fish, then transfer the skillet to the oven. Bake until the fish is nearly opaque, 7 to 10 minutes.

TO SERVE, spoon a generous dollop of mashed potatoes into the center of 6 individual plates. Drizzle some of the warm tomato coulis around the potatoes and set a portion of fish over the potatoes. Grind some pepper over the coulis and serve.

Makes 6 servings

PAN-SEARED HALIBUT CHEEKS
with Lemon-Chervil Beurre Blanc

Beach Side Cafe, West Vancouver, British Columbia

Halibut cheeks—those meaty, boneless delicacies—are preferred for this dish; however, the body meat of any firm white fish can be used, and scallops also work well. Chervil is a lacy-leafed herb resembling parsley, with a sweet, licorice flavor. The beurre blanc may separate if reheated, so it must be kept warm.

4 large halibut cheeks (about 8 ounces each), or smaller ones to total 2 pounds
½ cup all-purpose flour

2 tablespoons butter
2 tablespoons olive oil
Chervil sprigs, for garnish

LEMON-CHERVIL BEURRE BLANC

½ cup dry white wine
2 shallots, minced
1 clove garlic, minced
1 cup unsalted butter, chilled, cut in small pieces

Grated zest and juice of 1 lemon
¼ cup packed chervil leaves, rinsed, dried, and coarsely chopped
Salt and freshly ground white or black pepper

FOR THE BEURRE BLANC, combine the wine, shallots, and garlic in a small saucepan. Bring to a boil and boil until reduced by about half, 3 to 4 minutes. Remove the pan from the heat and whisk in the cold butter, a piece at a time, until all the butter is incorporated and the sauce has a creamy consistency. Stir in the lemon zest, lemon juice, and chervil, with salt and pepper to taste. Set aside in a warm spot, or over a pan of barely simmering water, until ready to use; do not let the sauce boil or it will separate.

SEASON THE HALIBUT cheeks with salt and pepper. Lightly coat them with flour, patting to remove excess. Heat the butter and olive oil together in a large, heavy skillet over medium-high heat. Add the halibut cheeks and cook until nicely browned, about 3 minutes on each side for medium, 4 to 5 minutes per side for fully cooked.

SPOON SOME of the beurre blanc onto 4 individual plates. Divide the halibut cheeks among the plates, setting them on the sauce. Garnish with the chervil sprigs and serve immediately.

Makes 4 servings

PESCADO ROJO
(Sole with Red Chile Garlic Salsa)

The Rio Cafe, Astoria, Oregon

Chile lovers will relish this fiery salsa flavored with roasted chiles and
lots of fresh garlic. The recipe is from the chef's family in Mexico. At the Rio Cafe,
this dish is served with pinto beans, Mexican rice, and homemade corn tortillas.
Any of our Northwest flounders will work nicely in this dish. Look for
petrale sole, lemon sole, or rex sole.

1 cup all-purpose flour
Salt and freshly ground black pepper
2 eggs
⅓ cup milk

2 cups finely ground cracker crumbs
  or bread crumbs
1½ pounds sole fillets
¼ cup vegetable oil (more if needed)

RED CHILE GARLIC SALSA

½ cup dried whole red chiles (chiles de arbol)
¾ cup boiling water
¼ cup chopped onion
5 cloves garlic
1 tablespoon coarsely chopped cilantro
1½ teaspoons paprika

1½ teaspoons ground cayenne
1½ teaspoons dried red pepper flakes
½ teaspoon chili powder
½ teaspoon salt
½ teaspoon lemon juice
½ teaspoon ground cumin

FOR THE SALSA, put the whole chiles in a dry, heavy skillet over high heat. When
hot, shake the pan so the chiles heat evenly; they should be about half blackened.
Immediately put the chiles in a bowl, pour the boiling water over them, and set aside
until lukewarm.

PUT THE CHILES and their soaking water in a food processor with the onion, garlic,
cilantro, paprika, cayenne, red pepper flakes, chili powder, salt, lemon juice, and cumin.
Process until well mixed but still slightly chunky. Set aside.

PUT THE FLOUR in a large, shallow dish and season generously with salt and pepper. Beat the eggs with the milk in a shallow bowl. Put the cracker crumbs in another large, shallow dish.

DIP A SOLE FILLET in the flour, patting to remove the excess. Then dip it into the egg mixture to coat. Finally, thoroughly dredge the fillet in the cracker crumbs, patting to remove the excess. Set aside on a plate lightly dusted with flour and repeat with the remaining fillets.

HEAT THE OIL in a large, heavy skillet over medium heat. Add the sole fillets and cook until golden brown, about 2 minutes. Turn the fish, then drizzle about 1 teaspoon of the salsa over each fillet. Continue cooking until the sole is just cooked through, about 2 minutes longer, depending on the thickness of the fillets. Transfer the sole to individual plates, passing the extra salsa separately. Serve immediately.

Makes 4 servings

SOLE AND FLOUNDER

Early on, U.S. fishmongers figured out that if they called flounder "sole," it sold much better than the same fish marketed as flounder. So here in the Pacific Northwest, fish known as "sole" is actually flounder unless it's been imported; the only true soles (such as Dover and thickback) are found in seas from the Mediterranean to Denmark.

The three most common varieties of sole sold in the Northwest are petrale sole, a large Pacific flounder found from the Mexican border north to Alaska; rex sole, a small Pacific flounder found from southern California to the Bering Sea; and lemon sole, a winter flounder weighing more than three pounds. These delicate-tasting fish are interchangeable in recipes.

Flounder and sole, along with plaice, halibut, and turbot, are known as flatfish. These bottom dwellers are distinguished by having both eyes on top of their heads. Many have the ability to change color when threatened, allowing them to blend unnoticeably into sand or rock.

Fillets vary in color, from white to ivory to gray, depending on the species. The meat of most sole is thin and delicate and should be cooked very quickly. When done, the fish will turn white and opaque.

BLACK COD SAKE KASU

Ray's Boathouse, Seattle, Washington

This exquisite sake kasu black cod is almost synonymous with Seattle's famed
Ray's Boathouse. Sake kasu is a thick paste made from the lees, or leftovers, from
the sake-fermenting process. It is available by the pound at Japanese specialty stores.
This preparation requires 48 hours to achieve its characteristic complex flavor,
so plan ahead. To match the flavors of this complex dish, serve an equally
complex wine, such as Ponzi Vineyards' Reserve Oregon Pinot Noir.

*2 to 2½ pounds black cod fillet, skin on, pin
bones removed, cut into 4 serving pieces
½ cup kosher or table salt, more if needed
6 ounces (¾ cup) kasu paste*

*⅓ cup sugar
¾ cup water
Fresh ginger, thinly sliced and blanched,
or pickled ginger, for serving*

SET THE BLACK COD pieces skin side down in a shallow dish. Sprinkle a generous
layer of salt over the fish, cover with plastic wrap, and refrigerate for 24 hours.

RINSE THE SALT from the fish and pat dry, then return the fish to the cleaned dish.

STIR TOGETHER the kasu paste and sugar in a small bowl until smooth. Slowly stir in
the water. Pour the kasu mixture evenly over the fish, cover, and refrigerate for another
24 hours.

BEFORE SERVING, light the coals in an outdoor grill. When the coals are very hot,
remove the black cod from the marinade, allowing the excess to drip off, and grill over
the hot coals until nicely browned and just cooked through, about 5 minutes per side.
Transfer the fish to individual plates, top with fresh or pickled ginger slices, and serve.

Makes 4 servings

Several different theories explain how our Northwest singing scallops got their name. Some credit it to the fact that, when steamed, their lovely pink, violet, and orange shells gape, giving them the appearance of someone singing. Others say it's because the scallops look like mouths singing in the water when they swim—which, like most scallops, they do by opening and closing their shells. Still others maintain that singing scallops used to be called swimming scallops and someone misunderstood the name.

What seafood lovers do know is that these colorful, delicately shelled scallops, indigenous to the waters of Puget Sound, Washington Sound, the Strait of Georgia, and the Strait of Juan de Fuca, are utterly delicious. Divers harvest wild singing scallops by hand. They are also farmed commercially in northern Washington and British Columbia.

As with clams, oysters, and mussels, the entire scallop (including the orange-colored "coral" or roe) is edible. Most Americans traditionally eat only the adductor muscle—the round, fleshy disk that opens and closes the shells. The rest of the scallop spoils rapidly and is usually discarded by processors. Because of their small size and delicate flavor, singing scallops are relished whole in the shell, either steamed or raw, often with their coral attached (which is also considered a delicacy).

Other Northwest scallops include the large weathervane sea scallop, the tiny Oregon bay scallop, and the giant purple-hinged rock scallop, which, unlike other scallops, is not free-swimming. Scallops cannot hold their shells firmly closed like other bivalves, and they quickly lose body moisture when removed from the water, so scallops in the shell must be very fresh. Shucked scallops will hold for a few days if well wrapped to prevent moisture loss. Scallops cook very quickly and are best slightly undercooked rather than overcooked.

Some processors soak sea scallops in sodium tripolyphosphates (STPP) to help prevent moisture loss. STPP also retards the growth of bacteria and removes any "fishy" odor. Unfortunately, this treatment results in a bland scallop that loses water during cooking. STPP-treated scallops are very white, are limp, have no odor, and stay separated in the package. Untreated scallops have a sweet sea odor, an ivory-yellow color, a firm texture, and a sticky coating that holds them together.

FILLET OF SOLE STUFFED WITH SHRIMP AND SCALLOPS

La Berengerie, Galiano Island, British Columbia

Colorful seafood roll-ups of snowy white sole, stuffed with a
speckled purée of Galiano Island shrimp and pink swimming (also known as singing)
scallops, are contrasted by a vivid orange sauce made with roasted red peppers.

2 red bell peppers	*4 ounces medium shrimp, peeled and deveined*
2 tablespoons olive oil	*¼ cup pine nuts*
1 medium onion, chopped	*¼ cup bread crumbs*
2 cloves garlic, minced	*2 tablespoons minced cilantro*
1 bay leaf	*2 tablespoons sour cream*
3 sprigs cilantro	*Salt and freshly ground black pepper*
1 cup white wine	*4 sole fillets (about 4 ounces each)*
1 pound swimming (singing) scallops in the shell, or 4 ounces bulk raw scallops	*¼ cup whipping cream*
	2 tablespoons capers

ROAST THE RED PEPPERS over a gas flame or under the broiler, turning often, until
evenly charred. Put the peppers in a paper or plastic bag, close the bag, and let sit until
cool enough to handle. Peel away and discard the skin, then halve the peppers, discarding
the cores and seeds. Set aside.

HEAT 1 TABLESPOON of the olive oil in a large saucepan. Add half the onion and
half the garlic and cook over medium heat, stirring, until fragrant, 2 to 3 minutes. Add
the bay leaf, cilantro sprigs, and wine. Bring just to a boil, add the singing scallops, cover
the pan, and cook until the scallops have opened, 6 to 8 minutes. (If using bulk scallops,
gently poach until just opaque, 3 to 5 minutes.) Remove the scallops and let cool for a
few minutes. Strain the cooking liquid and reserve (you should have about ¾ cup).

TAKE THE SCALLOPS from their shells, removing the black part and the vein on the side. Put the scallops in a food processor with the shrimp, pine nuts, bread crumbs, minced cilantro, sour cream, and half of 1 roasted red pepper. Process until just smooth, and season with a pinch each of salt and pepper.

PREHEAT THE OVEN to 350°F.

LAY THE SOLE FILLETS, smoother side up, on the work surface. Spread each fillet with about one-fourth of the stuffing and roll it up, beginning at the narrow end. Set the rolls, seam side down, in a lightly greased baking dish. Bake until opaque through (cut into 1 roll to test), about 20 minutes.

PREPARE THE SAUCE while the sole is baking. Heat the remaining 1 tablespoon olive oil in a medium saucepan. Add the remaining onion and garlic and cook over medium heat until fragrant, 2 to 3 minutes. Add the remaining roasted red peppers and the reserved scallop cooking liquid. Bring to a boil, reduce the heat, and simmer for 10 to 15 minutes. Let cool for about 10 minutes, then blend the mixture in a food processor or blender until smooth. Return the sauce to the pan and stir in the cream, adding salt and pepper to taste. Keep warm over low heat.

SET A STUFFED SOLE fillet on each of 4 individual plates, and spoon the sauce over and around them. Sprinkle the capers over the fillets and serve immediately.

Makes 4 servings

SEARED SEA SCALLOPS
with Huckleberry-Lavender Vinaigrette
and Chanterelle Salad

Columbia Gorge Hotel, Hood River, Oregon

"The stars of this recipe are three of the foods we are blessed with in the Northwest—seafood, wild mushrooms, and berries," says chef Britton Unketer. So of course, it's best to prepare this recipe in late summer or early fall, when chanterelle mushrooms are in season. Or use morel mushrooms as a spring substitute. Look for weathervane sea scallops, our largest Northwest scallop. (Note that the lavender oil needs to marinate for two hours.)

½ cup all-purpose flour	*1½ pounds sea scallops*
1 teaspoon freshly ground black pepper	*2 tablespoons vegetable oil*

HUCKLEBERRY-LAVENDER VINAIGRETTE

1 cup vegetable oil	*½ cup huckleberries (fresh or frozen)*
½ cup fresh or edible dried lavender,	*¼ cup white vinegar*
stems discarded, leaves and flowers minced	*Salt and freshly ground black pepper*

CHANTERELLE SALAD

2 tablespoons vegetable oil	*4 cups baby salad greens, rinsed and dried*
5 ounces chanterelle mushrooms, cleaned and trimmed, quartered if large	

FOR THE VINAIGRETTE, combine the oil and minced lavender in a small jar with a tight-fitting lid; shake well. Let the oil sit at room temperature for 2 hours, then strain off and discard the lavender. Return the oil to the jar. In a blender, purée the huckleberries with the vinegar until smooth. Strain the purée, then add it to the lavender oil, cover, and shake to mix well. Season to taste with salt and pepper and set aside.

FOR THE CHANTERELLE SALAD, heat the oil in a medium skillet over high heat, add the mushrooms, and sauté until just tender, 7 to 8 minutes. Transfer the mushrooms to a large bowl and add the salad greens and ⅓ cup of the vinaigrette. Toss gently to mix well. Season to taste with salt and pepper.

JUST BEFORE SERVING, combine the flour and pepper and lightly coat each scallop in the flour, patting to remove excess. Heat the oil in a large, heavy skillet or sauté pan over medium-high heat. Add the scallops and sear until nearly opaque, 4 to 5 minutes per side. Do not disturb the scallops while they cook, or they will not form the distinctive seared crust.

ARRANGE THE SCALLOPS around the outer edge of 4 individual plates, and pile the chanterelle salad in the center. Drizzle some of the remaining vinaigrette over the scallops and serve immediately.

Makes 4 servings

SOOKE TROUT BAKED IN PARCHMENT
with Spinach and Blackberry Sauce

The Good Life: A Bookstore and Cafe, Sooke, British Columbia

The parchment-paper envelope seals in all the fragrant juices of
leeks and trout. Look for parchment paper (sold in rolls or sheets) in kitchen stores
or the baking section of your grocery store. Waxed paper is not a substitute for
parchment paper; you can use foil, but it has less dramatic presentation appeal.

*1 cup blackberries
(fresh or unsweetened frozen)*
¼ cup blackberry vinegar or red wine vinegar
2 tablespoons minced shallot
1 bay leaf
1 cup white wine
½ cup fish stock (see page 83)
¼ cup whipping cream

1 cup finely shredded spinach leaves
1 to 2 teaspoons freshly squeezed lemon juice
*2 leeks, trimmed, washed, and cut in
    julienne strips*
1 tablespoon butter, melted
*8 small trout fillets (about 4 ounces each)
    or 4 large trout fillets (about 8
    ounces each)*

PASS THE BLACKBERRIES through a food mill or press through a sieve to remove
the seeds; you should have about ½ cup purée. Combine the vinegar, shallot, and bay
leaf in a small, heavy saucepan and boil until nearly all the liquid is evaporated. Add the
blackberry purée, wine, stock, and whipping cream, return to a simmer and reduce by
about half. Discard the bay leaf, stir in the spinach, and add salt and pepper to taste.
Continue cooking until the spinach is tender, 2 to 3 minutes longer. Purée the sauce in
a blender or food processor and return to the pan. Stir in lemon juice to taste and set
aside to keep warm.

PREHEAT THE OVEN to 425°F.

BRING A MEDIUM PAN of lightly salted water to a boil, add the leeks, and blanch until just tender, 1 to 2 minutes. Drain well and pat dry with paper towels.

CUT 4 LARGE PIECES of parchment paper about 24 inches long. Fold each in half, and trim the paper to a folded heart shape a couple of inches larger on all sides than a fillet. Lightly brush half of each heart with some of the butter and arrange a bed of leeks on the paper. Set the trout fillets on the leeks and season with salt and pepper. Fold the other half of the paper over the trout and make small folds along the edge of the paper to seal it. Set the packages on a baking sheet and bake until nicely browned and puffed, 6 to 8 minutes for 4-ounce trout fillets, 10 to 12 minutes for 8-ounce fillets.

SET EACH PACKAGE on a plate and tear open the top of the package. Drizzle some of the spinach and blackberry sauce over the fish and serve immediately.

Makes 4 servings

MARISCADA

La Margarita Co., Salem, Oregon

One whiff of this aromatic Mexican seafood stew is all you'll need to
whet your appetite. Good-quality locally made corn tortillas and a frosty
Northwest ale are the ideal accompaniments.

½ cup olive oil	*1 teaspoon dried oregano*
1 medium onion, chopped	*1 teaspoon ground chile de arbol or*
3 cloves garlic, chopped	*dried red pepper flakes*
1 yellow bell pepper, cored, seeded, and sliced	*Salt and freshly ground black pepper*
1 red bell pepper, cored, seeded, and sliced	*1 pound rockfish fillet, skin and pin bones*
1 green bell pepper, cored, seeded, and sliced	*removed, cut in 2-inch pieces*
1½ pounds tomatoes, cored and chopped	*1 pound clams, scrubbed*
½ pound crabmeat	*1 pound medium shrimp, peeled and deveined*
1 cup dry sherry or dry white wine	*½ pound mussels, cleaned and debearded*
1 teaspoon dried basil	*½ bunch cilantro leaves, chopped*

HEAT THE OIL in a large sauté pan over medium heat. Add the onion and garlic and
cook, stirring, until fragrant and beginning to soften, 3 to 4 minutes. Add the sliced bell
peppers and cook until tender, about 5 minutes longer. Add the tomatoes and cook until
the mixture is slightly thickened, about 10 minutes longer.

PICK OVER THE CRABMEAT to remove any bits of shell or cartilage.

STIR THE SHERRY, basil, oregano, and chile de arbol into the vegetables, with a
pinch each of salt and pepper. Simmer for 8 minutes. Add the rockfish, pressing it gently
into the sauce, and cook for 5 minutes longer. Gently stir in the clams, shrimp, mussels,
and crabmeat, cover the pan, and continue cooking until the seafood is just cooked, 6
to 8 minutes longer. Discard any clams or mussels that do not open. Spoon the stew into
individual bowls, sprinkle the cilantro over, and serve.

Makes 6 servings

STEAMER CLAMS

Three varieties of small, hard-shelled, sweet-tasting clams, commonly known as "steamer" clams, or "butter" clams, are available in the Northwest. All are delicious and they are interchangeable in recipes.

Native species include the littleneck clam (*Protothaca staminea*) and the Washington butter clam (*Saxidomus giganteus*). Littlenecks vary in color from cream to beige or gray. One variety is mottled with browns and yellows. Shells, averaging 2½ inches across, are crosshatched with growth rings crossing radiating ribs.

Washington butter clams have heavy, solid shells that are generally beige to gray in color. The shells grow from 3 to 4 inches across and are marked with concentric growth rings.

The most popular steamer clam on the market is the Manila clam (*Tapes japonica*), introduced to the Northwest from Asia in the 1930s. These oval-shaped clams, which range in size from 1½ to 2½ inches, have a ridged calico pattern on their shells.

Because the Manila clam cooks twice as fast as the native littleneck and butter clams (steaming time is just three to four minutes), this clam has become a favorite among Northwest chefs. Manilas are farmed throughout the world, with a significant commercial production in British Columbia and Washington.

Make sure clams are alive until cooking. The shell should be shut tight or should close tightly when tapped. Stored in refrigerator, covered with a damp cloth, live clams will keep three to five days.

CIOPPINO D'ORO

Bugatti's Ristorante, West Linn, Oregon

Chef Lydia Bugatti, who relies on the freshness of ingredients and on
cooking from the heart, offers her recipe for a spicy stew of Northwest seafood.
A rich, creamy white wine, such as a Chateau Ste. Michelle chardonnay, makes
a delightful companion for the sweet, complex seafood flavors of this cioppino.
You can streamline your shopping list by choosing just three or four of
the seafood varieties listed here, increasing their quantities slightly.

1 cup fish stock (see page 83) or chicken stock, (see page 81)	1 pound mussels, cleaned and debearded
2 pinches saffron threads	1 pound small clams, scrubbed
1 cup couscous	¾ pound salmon fillet, skin and pin bones removed, cut in 1-inch cubes
1 tablespoon olive oil	½ pound halibut or rockfish fillet, skin and pin bones removed, cut in 1-inch cubes
2 tablespoons chopped anchovies (about 1 can)	½ pound medium or large shrimp, peeled and deveined
½ teaspoon dried red pepper flakes	4 ounces bay scallops
1 tablespoon minced garlic	4 ounces cooked bay shrimp
¾ cup finely shredded basil leaves	Basil leaves, for garnish
¾ cup chopped plum (Roma) tomato	
1½ cups white wine	

HEAT THE STOCK in a small saucepan until warm, crush one pinch of the saffron
threads over it, remove from the heat, and let sit for 30 minutes. Bring the stock to a boil
and pour it over the couscous in a large serving bowl (the seafood will be added to this
bowl later). Cover the bowl and let sit for 5 minutes. Drizzle 1 teaspoon of the olive oil
over the couscous and stir with a fork to separate the grains and evenly coat them in oil.
Set aside.

HEAT THE REMAINING 2 teaspoons of olive oil in a large sauté pan or skillet over medium heat. Add the anchovies and sauté, stirring constantly, until they fall apart, 1 to 2 minutes. Stir in the dried red pepper flakes, garlic, basil, tomato, wine, and remaining pinch of saffron, in that order.

ADD THE MUSSELS and clams to the broth, cover the pan, and bring just to a boil. Lower the heat and simmer until the shellfish begin to open, 3 to 5 minutes. As they open, transfer the clams and mussels to the bowl with the couscous; cover the bowl to keep warm. When all the shellfish have opened (discard any that don't open after 10 minutes), add the salmon, halibut, raw shrimp, and scallops. Cover the pan and continue cooking until the seafood is just cooked through, 5 to 7 minutes, stirring in the bay shrimp at the last minute just to heat through. Taste the broth for seasoning. Carefully ladle the broth and seafood into the bowl with the couscous, garnish with basil leaves, and serve.

Makes 4 to 6 servings

BLACK MUSSEL FETTUCCINE
in Scotch Whisky Cream

McCormick's Fish House and Bar, Seattle, Washington

The peaty, smoky essence of Scotch whisky permeates this delicious
pasta. Crusty bread and a garden tomato salad complete the meal. To balance
the smoky richness of the cream sauce, try a Hogue Cellars fumé blanc.

1 pound dried fettuccine	1 to 2 pounds mussels, cleaned and debearded
1 tablespoon olive oil	2 cups whipping cream
½ cup sliced mushrooms	2 tablespoons minced green onions
1 teaspoon minced shallot	1 teaspoon Dijon-style mustard
1 teaspoon minced garlic	Salt and freshly ground black pepper
⅓ cup Scotch whisky	

BRING A LARGE POT of salted water to a boil.

HEAT THE OLIVE OIL in a large saucepan and add the mushrooms, shallot, and garlic.
Sauté until the mushrooms begin to soften. Add the Scotch and tilt the pan so the liquid
settles to one side, warming it for just a moment. Light a match and carefully draw it to
the pan just until the Scotch lights; let burn until the flame subsides. Stir in the mussels
with the cream, green onions, and mustard. Simmer until the mussels have opened, 5 to
7 minutes, transferring them to a bowl as they open; discard any mussels that do not open.
Taste the sauce for seasoning. If the sauce is not thick enough to coat a spoon, boil to
reduce it.

WHEN THE WATER BOILS, add the fettuccine and cook until al dente, 5 to 7 minutes.
Drain well and put the fettuccine in a large serving bowl. Pour the mussels and sauce
over the pasta; toss to coat well. Serve family style from the bowl at the table, or arrange
on individual plates, distributing the mussels evenly. Serve immediately.

Makes 4 servings

GRILLED CRAB AND CHEDDAR SANDWICH

Tokeland Hotel & Restaurant, Tokeland, Washington

Nothing showcases Northwest Dungeness crab better than simplicity.
Here's a standout sandwich that needs nothing more than
a crank of freshly ground black pepper.

2 cups crabmeat (about ¾ pound)	8 slices sourdough bread
2 cups grated sharp cheddar cheese	3 tablespoons butter, melted (more if needed)
4 to 5 tablespoons mayonnaise	

PICK OVER the crabmeat to remove any bits of shell or cartilage.

COMBINE THE CRABMEAT and cheese in a large bowl and stir to mix. Add enough mayonnaise to hold the mixture together.

SPREAD THE CRAB MIXTURE on 4 slices of the bread and top with the remaining bread. Brush the tops with some of the melted butter. Heat a heavy skillet or griddle over medium heat. Add the sandwiches, buttered side down, and toast until browned, about 2 minutes. Brush the tops with more butter, turn the sandwiches, and continue toasting until the second side is browned and the cheese has melted, 2 to 3 minutes longer.

TRANSFER THE SANDWICHES to individual plates and serve, cut in half if desired.

Makes 4 servings

LINGUINE WITH CRAWFISH
AND FIRE SAUCE

Jake's Famous Crayfish Restaurant, Portland, Oregon

Northwest crawfish (or crayfish), a freshwater relative of the lobster,
were first served by Jake's namesake, "Jake" Freiman, at the old Oregon
Hotel in 1881. Freiman guaranteed the freshest possible crawfish by keeping an
inventory thriving in small ponds he had dug in the restaurant's basement. Most
crawfish, however, thrive in Northwest rivers and lake bottoms, with the
largest specimens harvested from the Columbia River. Aficionados insist
that our Northwest crawfish are the sweetest tasting around.

¼ cup butter	½ cup diced red bell pepper
1 pound crawfish tail meat	½ cup diced red onion
2 teaspoons minced garlic	½ cup chicken stock (see page 81)
2 teaspoons minced shallot	12 ounces dried linguine
2 cups corn kernels	¼ cup grated Parmesan cheese
½ cup diced green bell pepper	

FIRE SAUCE

2 red bell peppers	1 teaspoon minced jalapeño pepper
4 ounces cream cheese	½ teaspoon ground pasilla chile
2 tablespoons grated cheddar cheese	or other ground chile
1½ tablespoons canned chipotle chiles	¼ teaspoon ground cumin
4 cloves garlic, coarsely chopped	¼ teaspoon Cajun seasoning
2 teaspoons minced shallot	Salt

FOR THE FIRE SAUCE, roast the red peppers over a gas flame or under the broiler,
turning often, until evenly charred. Put the peppers in a paper or plastic bag, close the
bag, and let sit until cool enough to handle. Peel away and discard the skin, then halve
the peppers, discarding the cores and seeds. Set aside.

COMBINE THE ROASTED red peppers with the cream cheese, cheddar cheese, chipotles, garlic, shallot, jalapeño, pasilla, cumin, and Cajun seasoning in a food processor or blender and process until smooth. Season to taste with salt and set aside.

BRING A LARGE SAUCEPAN of lightly salted water to a boil.

HEAT THE BUTTER in a large sauté pan, add the crawfish, garlic, and shallot, and sauté, stirring, for 1 to 2 minutes. Stir in the corn, peppers, and onion and season to taste with salt and pepper. Continue cooking until the vegetables are just tender, 3 to 4 minutes longer. Add the chicken stock and the fire sauce and stir until heated through.

WHEN THE WATER BOILS, add the linguine and cook until al dente, 5 to 7 minutes. Drain well and put the pasta in a large bowl. Pour the sauce over the pasta, toss well, and arrange the pasta on 4 individual plates, distributing the crawfish evenly. Sprinkle each plate with the Parmesan cheese and serve.

Makes 4 servings

DUNGENESS CRAB CAKES

Avalon Grill, Portland, Oregon

Here's a fun twist to a Northwest classic: sweet, succulent Dungeness crab with poblano chiles and a robust sun-dried tomato remoulade. Enjoy this dish with a melony chardonnay from Silver Lake.

1 tablespoon olive oil	¾ cup bread crumbs (more if needed)
¾ cup minced yellow onion	¼ cup whipping cream
¾ cup minced red onion	1 egg, separated
1 small yellow bell pepper, cored, seeded, and finely chopped	Hot pepper sauce
	Salt and freshly ground pepper, preferably white
½ poblano chile, cored, seeded, and finely chopped	½ cup all-purpose flour
1 pound Dungeness crabmeat	¼ cup vegetable oil, for frying

SUN-DRIED TOMATO REMOULADE

1 cup mayonnaise	1 tablespoon minced red onion
¼ cup mustard, preferably Creole style	1 tablespoon minced flat-leaf (Italian) parsley
¼ cup minced celery	1 tablespoon paprika
¼ cup minced sun-dried tomatoes (oil-packed variety)	½ teaspoon salt
2 tablespoons minced red or green bell pepper	¼ teaspoon freshly ground pepper, preferably white
2 tablespoons minced green onion	

FOR THE REMOULADE, combine the mayonnaise, mustard, celery, tomatoes, red or green bell pepper, green onion, red onion, parsley, paprika, salt, and pepper in a bowl and whisk together until thoroughly mixed. Taste for seasoning and refrigerate until needed.

HEAT THE OLIVE OIL in a large skillet, add the onions, yellow bell pepper, and chile, and cook over medium heat, stirring occasionally, until the onions are translucent, 3 to 5 minutes. Transfer the mixture to a colander and let cool for about 20 minutes, allowing excess liquid to drain off.

REMOVE ANY BITS of shell or cartilage from the crabmeat.

IN A LARGE BOWL, combine the sautéed vegetables with the crabmeat, bread crumbs, whipping cream, and egg yolk. Stir gently to mix, adding hot pepper sauce, salt, and pepper to taste.

PUT THE EGG WHITE in a shallow bowl and lightly beat it; put the flour on a plate. Form the crab mixture into 12 cakes of about ¼ cup each. Dip the cakes into the egg white and then thoroughly coat them with flour, patting to remove the excess.

HEAT THE VEGETABLE OIL in a deep, heavy skillet over medium heat. Fry the crab cakes in batches until nicely browned, 2 to 3 minutes per side. Let drain briefly on paper towels, then arrange 2 cakes on each of 6 individual plates. Spoon some of the tomato remoulade alongside the crab cakes, and pass the rest separately.

Makes 6 servings

SEAFOOD PASTA
in White Wine Butter Sauce

The Captain's Palace, Victoria, British Columbia

Brimming with flavors of the sea, this colorful pasta is simple and stunning.
Match with a crisp, fruity Northwest chardonnay.

12 ounces dried linguine

3 tablespoons vegetable oil

*¾ pound salmon fillet, skin and pin bones
removed, cut in 1-inch pieces*

*¾ pound halibut fillet, skin and pin bones
removed, cut in 1-inch pieces*

½ pound clams, scrubbed

½ pound mussels, cleaned and debearded

*½ pound medium shrimp,
peeled and deveined*

1½ cups white wine

½ cup minced onion

*1 red bell pepper, cored, seeded,
and cut in thin strips*

*4 ounces mushrooms, cleaned,
trimmed, and sliced*

1 tablespoon minced garlic

Pinch dried red pepper flakes, or to taste

¼ cup butter, cut in pieces and chilled

Salt and freshly ground black pepper

*Grated Asiago or Parmesan cheese,
for serving (optional)*

BRING A LARGE POT of lightly salted water to a boil, add the linguine, and cook
until just tender, 3 to 5 minutes. Drain well and toss with 1 tablespoon of the oil to keep
from sticking together. Set aside and keep warm.

HEAT THE REMAINING 2 tablespoons oil in a large skillet or sauté pan. Add the
salmon and halibut and cook over medium heat until about half cooked, 2 to 3 minutes.
Add the clams, mussels, shrimp, wine, onion, bell pepper, mushrooms, garlic, and red pepper flakes. Cover the pan and continue cooking until the clams and mussels are open and
the shrimp are just cooked through, 3 to 5 minutes. Remove the lid, add the butter, and
gently swirl the pan until the butter has melted. Season to taste with salt and pepper.

ARRANGE THE WARM PASTA in 4 individual soup plates or wide bowls, with clams
and mussels around the edge. Spoon the fish, vegetables, and sauce over the pasta, with
the shrimp on top. Sprinkle with grated cheese, if using, and serve immediately.

Makes 4 servings

ASPARAGUS GIOVANNI

Giovanni's on Pearl, Ellensburg, Washington

"We put this on our menu in the spring, when fresh Yakima Valley asparagus is abundant," says the chef of Giovanni's on Pearl, who serves this vegetarian entrée with crusty French bread and butter. Contrary to what many people believe, thick asparagus spears are often more tender than thin ones. In fact, tenderness has to do with age and moisture content, not size.

1 pound dried fettuccine or other pasta	*4 cloves garlic, chopped, or more to taste*
1 teaspoon salt	*1 teaspoon fennel seeds, crushed*
1¼ pounds asparagus, trimmed and	*Pinch dried red pepper flakes*
cut in 1-inch lengths	*6 basil leaves, finely chopped*
1 cup sliced regular or wild mushrooms	*Salt and freshly ground black pepper*
(about 2 ounces)	*2 tablespoons butter*
½ cup dry white wine	*¼ to ½ cup grated Parmesan or*
¼ cup olive oil	*Romano cheese*

BRING A LARGE POT of salted water to a boil, add the pasta, and cook until al dente, about 8 to 10 minutes.

WHILE THE PASTA is cooking, combine the asparagus, mushrooms, wine, olive oil, garlic, fennel seeds, and pepper flakes in a skillet and bring just to a boil. Reduce the heat and simmer, partly covered, until the asparagus is just tender but still crisp and most of the liquid has evaporated, about 10 minutes. (If the liquid evaporates before the asparagus is cooked, add a tablespoon of water.) When the asparagus is cooked, stir in the basil, adding salt and pepper to taste.

WHEN THE PASTA is cooked, drain well and return it to the pot. Add the butter to the hot pasta and toss to coat well. Arrange the pasta on 4 warmed plates and top with the asparagus and sauce. Sprinkle with Parmesan cheese and serve.

Makes 4 servings

QUINOA-STUFFED DELICATA SQUASH

Nearly Normal's, Corvallis, Oregon

Quinoa (pronounced "*keen*-wa") is a tiny, milletlike seed
that is cooked much like other grains. It is available in most health food stores.
Delicata is a sweet, smooth-textured squash. If you can't find it, substitute
another variety, such as acorn squash.

3 Delicata squash (about 1 pound each)	*4 teaspoons minced garlic, or to taste*
1½ cups quinoa	*1 tablespoon minced fresh marjoram,*
3 cups water	*or 1½ teaspoons dried*
½ teaspoon salt	*¼ teaspoon ground cardamom*
2 tablespoons vegetable oil	*Salt*
1 cup finely chopped celery	*1½ cups grated fontina or*
1 cup finely chopped onion	*other semi-soft cheese*
½ cup finely chopped red bell pepper	

PREHEAT THE OVEN to 375°F.

HALVE THE SQUASH lengthwise and scoop out and discard the seeds. Set the squash
cut side down in a roasting pan or rimmed baking sheet. Add ¼ inch of water to the pan
and bake the squash until tender when pierced with a fork, 20 to 30 minutes (other
types of squash may take longer). Leave the oven set at 375°F.

WHILE THE SQUASH BAKES, put the quinoa in a medium saucepan with the water and salt. Bring to a boil, reduce the heat, and simmer, covered, until all the water has been absorbed, about 15 minutes. Set aside.

HEAT THE OIL in a large saucepan. Add the celery, onion, bell pepper, garlic, marjoram, and cardamom and sauté, stirring, until tender, about 5 minutes. Remove from the heat, stir in the quinoa, and add salt to taste.

SET THE SQUASH cut side up on a dry baking sheet. Fill each half with the quinoa mixture and sprinkle the grated cheese on top. Bake until the filling is bubbly and lightly browned, 15 to 18 minutes. Serve immediately.

Makes 6 servings

PASTA WITH GRILLED EGGPLANT AND ONION

Cafe Luna, Shelton, Washington

Grilled eggplant has an alluring sweet, smoky flavor and a seductive
meaty texture. In this recipe it's tossed with aromatic herbs, to create a delicious
topping for pasta. To enhance the rich flavors of this dish, pour Hogue Cellars'
supple, rich merlot, smacking of intense berry flavors and lively spice.

2 eggplants (about 2 pounds total),	*½ cup extra-virgin olive oil*
sliced ½ inch thick	*¼ cup balsamic vinegar*
3 red onions, sliced ½ inch thick	*Salt and freshly ground black pepper*
½ cup chopped basil	*1½ pounds dried fettuccine or*
½ cup chopped mint	*other broad pasta*
4 cloves garlic, minced	*Sprigs of basil, mint, and/or flat-leaf (Italian)*
½ teaspoon dried red pepper flakes	*parsley, for garnish*

LAY THE EGGPLANT slices on a baking sheet and liberally sprinkle both sides with
salt; let sit for 15 to 20 minutes (this draws out excess moisture along with any bitterness
the eggplant may have). Wipe off the salt and pat dry.

LIGHT THE COALS in an outdoor grill or preheat the broiler. Grill or broil the eggplant and onion slices until just tender, 6 to 8 minutes, turning occasionally. Let cool
slightly, then coarsely chop.

COMBINE THE EGGPLANT, onion, basil, mint, garlic, and red pepper flakes and toss to mix. In a small bowl, whisk together the olive oil and balsamic vinegar and pour over the vegetables. Toss to coat well and season to taste with salt and pepper. Let stand at least 1 hour.

JUST BEFORE SERVING, bring a large pot of lightly salted water to a boil, add the pasta, and cook until al dente, about 5 minutes. Drain well and arrange the pasta on individual plates. Spoon the vegetables over the pasta, garnish with the herb sprigs, and serve.

Makes 6 to 8 servings

CHANTERELLE RISOTTO CAKES

Bay Cafe, Lopez Island, Washington

At the Bay Cafe, these savory wild chanterelle and rice cakes are served
alongside filet mignon or grilled shrimp. But topped with sautéed mushrooms,
they would also make a fine main course.

5 cups chicken stock (see page 81)
½ cup dry white wine
2 tablespoons minced flat-leaf (Italian) parsley
3 tablespoons olive oil
4 tablespoons unsalted butter (more if needed)
1 bunch green onions, minced

2 cloves garlic, minced
*½ pound golden chanterelle mushrooms,
    cleaned, trimmed, and thinly sliced*
1½ cups arborio rice
½ cup grated Parmesan cheese
Salt and freshly ground black pepper

GARNISH

1 cup finely shredded spinach leaves
½ cup grated Parmesan cheese

¼ cup toasted pine nuts

COMBINE THE STOCK, wine, and parsley in a medium saucepan and bring just to a
low simmer.

HEAT THE OLIVE OIL and 3 tablespoons of the butter in a large, heavy skillet over
medium heat. Add the green onions and garlic and sauté until beginning to soften, about
3 minutes. Add the chanterelles and continue sautéing until the mushrooms have released
their juices, stirring often, 4 to 5 minutes longer. Stir in the rice until it is evenly glossy.

ADD 1 CUP of the hot stock to the rice and cook over medium heat, stirring constantly, until all of the liquid is absorbed. Continue adding stock, 1 cup at a time, about every 5 minutes, allowing the rice to absorb each addition before adding the next. When all the stock has been absorbed and the rice is tender, remove the pan from the heat and stir in the Parmesan cheese. Season to taste with salt and pepper and let cool.

WHEN COOL, FORM the risotto into cakes, using ½ cup for each, and making them about 3½ inches across and ½ inch thick. Lay the cakes on a baking sheet lined with plastic wrap, cover with a second sheet of plastic wrap, and refrigerate for 2 hours.

JUST BEFORE SERVING, heat the remaining 1 tablespoon butter in a large skillet, preferably nonstick. When the butter is melted and begins to foam, add some of the risotto cakes in a single layer; do not crowd the pan. Cook the cakes over medium-high heat until well browned and crusty, about 3 minutes on each side. Transfer the risotto cakes to a platter and keep warm while frying the remaining cakes, adding more butter as needed.

ARRANGE THE RISOTTO cakes on plates, sprinkle with spinach, Parmesan cheese, and pine nuts, and serve.

Makes 4 to 6 servings

PUMPKIN GNOCCHI
in Roasted Vegetable Pesto Cream Sauce

Il Piatto, Portland, Oregon

Delicately colored and flavored with pumpkin, these tender potato dumplings (gnocchi) are served in a cream sauce flavored with a sweet, earthy roasted vegetable pesto. Any leftover pesto can be saved for the next day's pasta.

2 pounds baking potatoes, scrubbed	*½ cup pumpkin purée*
2 teaspoons butter	*(fresh cooked or canned)*
1 cup chopped onion	*2 eggs*
2 tablespoons chopped garlic	*1 tablespoon salt*
3 cups all-purpose flour,	*1 teaspoon ground nutmeg*
plus extra for rolling gnocchi	

ROASTED VEGETABLE PESTO

½ pound carrots, peeled, halved if large	*½ cup grated Asiago cheese*
½ pound onions, peeled and quartered	*3 tablespoons minced garlic*
3 red bell peppers, cored, seeded, and quartered	*Salt and freshly ground black pepper*
¾ cup olive oil	*2 cups half-and-half*

PREHEAT THE OVEN to 400°F.

FOR THE ROASTED VEGETABLE PESTO, arrange the carrot, onion, and red pepper in a baking dish and drizzle about ¼ cup of the olive oil over them. Roast the vegetables until lightly browned and tender, about 30 minutes.

TRANSFER THE VEGETABLES to a food processor and process until very smooth. With the machine running, slowly pour in the remaining ½ cup olive oil, then add the cheese and garlic. Season to taste with salt and pepper; set aside.

PUT THE POTATOES in a large pan with lightly salted water to cover. Bring to a boil and simmer until the potatoes are tender when pierced with a knife, 20 to 30 minutes, depending on their size.

WHILE THE POTATOES are cooking, heat the butter in a medium skillet, add the onion and garlic, and sauté over medium heat, stirring frequently, until tender, about 5 minutes.

DRAIN THE POTATOES and let sit until cool enough to handle. Peel away the skin and purée the potatoes in a ricer or with a potato masher. Stir in the sautéed onion and garlic with the flour, pumpkin, eggs, salt, and nutmeg. Stir until well mixed, then knead the mixture to form a smooth dough, 1 to 2 minutes.

LIGHTLY FLOUR your hands and the work surface. Break off a large piece of dough and roll it into a cylinder about ½ inch in diameter. Slice ½ inch thick and set the gnocchi aside on a tray lined with parchment paper or foil. Repeat with the remaining dough.

BRING THE HALF-AND-HALF to a boil in a medium skillet. Add the vegetable pesto and season to taste with salt and pepper. Set aside, covered, to keep warm.

BRING A LARGE PAN of salted water to a boil and gently drop in the gnocchi, a handful at a time. Simmer the gnocchi until they rise to the surface, 2 to 3 minutes. Scoop them out with a slotted spoon and put them in a large bowl of cold water. Continue cooking the remaining gnocchi.

DRAIN THE COOKED gnocchi well, add them to the warm sauce, and simmer for a few minutes to heat through. Transfer to a serving bowl or individual plates and serve immediately.

Makes 6 to 8 servings

DESSERTS

NOOTKA ROSE PETAL ICE CREAM

Friday Harbor House, San Juan Island, Washington

During the summer months, San Juan Island erupts with a festival of flowers. None are more fragrant than the tiny native Nootka rose, with its compelling, spicy scent. Not all rose petals can create the delicate flavor of this ice cream; they must be richly aromatic. If you can't gather your own wild rose petals, chef Greg Atkinson recommends using unsprayed dried rosebuds from France, sold at specialty stores throughout the Northwest.

2 cups milk	*6 egg yolks*
2 cups fresh, unsprayed fragrant rose petals	*1 cup sugar*
or ⅔ cup dried	*2 cups whipping cream, chilled*

COMBINE THE MILK and rose petals in a saucepan and bring to a boil over medium heat. As soon as the milk boils, remove the pan from the heat; let stand for 10 minutes.

STIR TOGETHER the egg yolks and sugar in a medium bowl. Strain the milk into the yolk mixture, stirring to mix. Discard the rose petals and wipe out the pan if necessary. Return the mixture to the saucepan and cook over medium-low heat until the custard is thick enough to coat the back of a spoon, 5 to 7 minutes. Do not let the custard boil or it will curdle.

LET THE CUSTARD COOL slightly, then refrigerate until chilled. Stir in the chilled cream, pour the mixture into an ice cream maker, and freeze according to the manufacturer's instructions. Transfer the frozen ice cream to an airtight freezer container and freeze for at least 1 hour before serving.

Makes about 1½ quarts

ESPRESSO CRÈME BRÛLÉE
with Espresso Cookies

Fullers, Seattle, Washington

Where else but Seattle? A dessert with a jolt.

The best tool for caramelizing the tops of crème brûlée is a blowtorch:
the flame caramelizes the sugar without heating the custard. You can also
caramelize the tops under a broiler. Both the custard and the cookie dough need to
chill for a few hours in the refrigerator, so plan ahead. They can be prepared up to
several days in advance, though you will need to caramelize the custard tops just
before serving. The cookie recipe makes a generous amount; slice off what
you need, rewrap the dough, and refrigerate the rest for later.

6 egg yolks	*1½ cups whipping cream*
¾ cup sugar, plus about 6 tablespoons	*½ cup half-and-half*
more for caramelizing	*½ vanilla bean, split,*
½ cup strong espresso	*or 1 teaspoon vanilla extract*

ESPRESSO COOKIES

1 cup unsalted butter, softened	*1¾ cups sifted all-purpose flour*
½ cup sugar	*Pinch salt*
¼ cup finely ground espresso beans	

FOR THE COOKIES, cream the butter and sugar until fluffy. Add the ground espresso,
flour, and salt and blend well. Form the dough into a log 2 inches in diameter and
wrap it in waxed paper, foil, or plastic wrap, twisting the ends firmly to snugly enclose
the dough. Chill the cookie dough for at least 2 hours before baking.

PREHEAT THE OVEN to 300°F.

FOR THE CRÈME BRÛLÉE, blend the egg yolks and sugar together in a bowl. Warm the espresso, stirring until the sugar is dissolved. Add the cream and half-and-half. Scrape the seeds from the vanilla bean with a small knife, add them to the pan (or stir in the vanilla extract), and stir until thoroughly combined; discard the rest of the vanilla bean.

POUR THE CUSTARD mixture into six ½-cup crème brûlée dishes or ramekins and set them in a large baking pan. Add boiling water to the pan to reach halfway up the sides of the dishes. Bake until the custard is set, about 40 minutes. To test whether the custard is done, insert the tip of a knife in the center; it should come out clean. Remove the custards from the pan, let cool, then refrigerate.

JUST BEFORE SERVING, preheat the oven to 350°F. Unwrap the cookie dough and cut twelve ¼-inch-thick slices. Set the slices on a baking sheet with at least 1 inch between them. Bake until just lightly browned, 8 to 10 minutes.

SPRINKLE THE TOP of each custard with about 1 tablespoon of sugar. Caramelize the sugar with a blowtorch or under a very hot broiler. Serve immediately, with the espresso cookies.

Makes 6 servings

CRANBERRY-APPLE BETTE

Wharfside Bed & Breakfast, Friday Harbor, Washington

Serve this tangy cranberry "bette" warm from the oven for dessert (or even breakfast). Tart, firm apples, such as Granny Smiths, Fujis, or Gravensteins, are recommended.

6 tablespoons butter	*1 cup packed brown sugar*
4 cups finely cubed soft bread, preferably	*¾ teaspoon ground nutmeg*
Seattle sourdough	*½ teaspoon ground cinnamon*
5 cups peeled, sliced baking apples	*2 cups cranberries (fresh or thawed frozen)*
(4 to 5 large apples)	

LEMON SAUCE

½ cup granulated sugar	*1 teaspoon grated lemon zest*
1 tablespoon cornstarch	*2 tablespoons freshly squeezed lemon juice*
Pinch salt	*2 tablespoons butter*
1 cup water	

HEAT 3 TABLESPOONS of the butter in a large skillet over medium-high heat, add the bread cubes, and cook, stirring often, until the bread is browned, about 4 to 5 minutes. Set aside.

PREHEAT THE OVEN to 350°F.

ARRANGE HALF of the apple slices in a greased 8-inch square baking dish. In a small bowl, stir together the brown sugar, nutmeg, and cinnamon. Sprinkle half of the sugar mixture over the apples and top with half of the bread cubes. Dot the bread with 1½ tablespoons of the remaining butter, and spread the cranberries on top. Layer with the remaining apple slices, followed by the remaining sugar mixture, then the remaining bread cubes. Dot the top with the remaining 1½ tablespoons butter, cover the dish with foil, and bake for 45 minutes. Remove the foil and use the back of a spoon to press gently on the topping so that it soaks up some of the juices below. Continue baking until the top is golden brown, 15 to 20 minutes longer.

PREPARE THE LEMON SAUCE while the betty is baking. Stir together the sugar, cornstarch, and salt in a small saucepan. Add the water and lemon zest and bring to a boil. Simmer the sauce until slightly thickened, about 2 minutes. Remove from the heat, add the lemon juice and butter, and stir until the butter is melted.

WHEN THE BETTY IS DONE, remove it from the oven and let it sit for 5 minutes. Spoon the betty onto individual plates or bowls and serve warm with the lemon sauce drizzled over it.

Makes 6 to 8 servings

CRANBERRIES: FROM THE BOG TO THE TABLE

Each autumn the Long Beach Peninsula in Southwest Washington is ablaze in scarlet and crimson as acres of cranberries hang red, ripe, and ready for harvest. Cranberries have been raised commercially on the peninsula for over 100 years, and growers there now raise more than five million pounds of cranberries annually. Long before the commercial harvest, Native Americans gathered wild cranberries, which grew in local peat bogs and muskegs. They steam-cooked the berries or stored them in damp moss, and then pounded and mixed them with deer or elk meat and fat to make pemmican, a high-calorie food for traveling. Later, cranberries became an important trade item with early Northwest settlers.

Originally called craneberries, because the flower resembles the bill of a crane, cranberries are a low-growing member of the heath family, which also includes blueberries and salal. Most cranberries from the Long Beach Peninsula are raised and sold to cranberry giant Ocean Spray of Massachusetts.

Because of their high pectin content, cranberries jell nicely. They are packed with vitamin C, a fact known to old-time New England sea captains, who stocked them aboard ship to prevent scurvy. One-half cup of unsweetened whole cranberries contains only about 20 calories. The color in cranberries has to do with their variety, not quality.

After purchasing cranberries, sort them without washing and place in a bowl or glass jar. Cover loosely and refrigerate. Wash just before using.

CHOCOLATE SOUFFLÉ TARTS

Bugatti's Ristorante, West Linn, Oregon

Topped with a fluffy cloud of barely sweet whipped cream and
warm bittersweet chocolate sauce, these intensely flavored individual chocolate
soufflés are a sophisticated dessert indulgence.

1¼ cups sugar	3 whole eggs, separated
½ cup milk	2 egg whites
7 ounces high-quality unsweetened chocolate,	Pinch cream of tartar
such as Callebaut or Valrhona, coarsely chopped	

WHIPPED CREAM

1 cup whipping cream	1 teaspoon sugar

WARM CHOCOLATE SAUCE

4 ounces high-quality semisweet chocolate,	½ cup whipping cream
such as Callebaut or Valrhona,	
coarsely chopped	

PREHEAT THE OVEN to 400°F.

HEAT 1 CUP of the sugar with the milk in a medium saucepan until the sugar
has dissolved, stirring occasionally. Bring just to a boil, add the unsweetened chocolate,
remove from the heat, and stir until the chocolate is melted. Let cool for 10 minutes.

LIGHTLY GREASE eight 4-inch tartlet tins and set them on a baking sheet.

BEAT THE 5 EGG WHITES with the cream of tartar until soft peaks form. Add the remaining ¼ cup sugar, and continue beating until stiff and glossy.

STIR THE EGG YOLKS into the chocolate mixture, then gently fold the chocolate into the egg whites, a third at a time. Pour the batter into the prepared tartlet tins, filling them to about ¼ inch from the top. Bake until puffed and the tops start to split, 12 to 15 minutes; do not open the oven door during cooking.

WHILE THE TARTS are baking, whip the cream with the 1 teaspoon of sugar until soft peaks form. Chill until needed.

FOR THE CHOCOLATE SAUCE, combine the semisweet chocolate and cream in a small saucepan and warm over low heat, stirring often, until the chocolate has melted and the sauce is smooth. Keep warm.

LET THE TARTS sit for a few minutes before unmolding. Set them on individual plates, drizzle the warm chocolate sauce over them, and top each tart with a dollop of whipped cream. Serve immediately.

Makes 8 servings

Blackberries

Himalaya blackberry *(Rubus procerus)*: The Himalaya blackberry, originally a cultivated variety, has become naturalized in the Northwest and is the most prolific of our "wild" blackberries. This is a large, juicy, flavorful berry, but when cooked it is rather bland unless you add lemon juice.

Pacific trailing wild blackberry or dewberry *(R. ursinus)*: Often found growing in areas where the ground has been disturbed, this tiny, superb native berry is more flavorful and has fewer seeds than the Himalaya or evergreen blackberries.

Evergreen blackberry *(R. laciniatus)*: Also an escapee from cultivation, this plant has deeply toothed leaves. Its berries are more round and compact than those of the Himalaya variety and have a less complex flavor.

Cultivated blackberries: Blackberry hybrids include the marionberry, loganberry, tayberry, boysenberry, and Kakota berry (a new cross developed at Oregon State University). These hybrids tend to be larger and less seedy than their wild cousins.

Raspberries

Wild raspberry *(R. idaeus)*: These flavorful berries are a bit smaller than cultivated raspberries and grow in shades of red or yellow.

Black raspberry or blackcap *(R. leucodemis)*: This native shrub has a distinctive blue-gray bloom on the fruit and stalks. The blackish-purple berries are soft and have a distinctive, Muscat-like flavor.

Thimbleberry *(R. parviflorus)*: A shallow-cupped, soft, scarlet berry with a very sweet flavor, the thimbleberry should be used as soon as possible after picking.

Salmonberry *(R. spectabilis)*: These large, fleshy berries vary from salmon and gold to deep crimson and maroon. Depending on where they grow, the flavor ranges from insipid to very sweet.

Cultivated raspberries: Varieties popular in the Northwest include Willamette and Meeker (a juicy early-ripening variety).

Strawberries

Several varieties of wild strawberries are native to the Northwest. All are low-growing shrubs with tiny, edible berries. The most flavorful is the coastal strawberry, *Fragaria chiloensis*.

The larger hybrid strawberries were first developed in the 1800s, when the large South American variety was crossed with the smaller European variety. Unlike the stalwart strawberries imported from California and New Zealand, which are bred for hardiness and are often insipid, Northwest strawberry varieties, which include Hood, Totem, Rainier, and Shuksan, are juicy and deep red throughout.

Blueberries and Their Relatives

Most wild members of the blueberry family can be substituted for cultivated blueberries in your favorite recipe.

Salal berry *(Gaultheria shallon)*: These large, dark-blue to violet berries have a sweet blueberry flavor with a refreshing minty aftertaste (salal is closely related to the wintergreen plant). Northwest natives ate salal with a special spoon made of black mountain goat horn that did not show the berry stains.

Oval-leaved blueberry *(Vaccinium ovalifolium)*: Found in deep woods at middle elevations, these round, blue berries are covered with a soft, gray bloom. They are sweet and flavorful.

Evergreen huckleberry *(V. ovatum)*: Found along the coast and in the foothills, these shiny, purple-to-blue-black berries are packed with flavor.

Wild mountain huckleberry or black huckleberry *(V. membranaceum)*: These shiny, pear-shaped blue-black berries grow in the foothills at elevations above 3,000 feet. They are highly prized for baking and even winemaking.

Red huckleberry *(V. parvifolium)*: Translucent rose to candy-apple red, these tart berries are delicious in pies, muffins, and pancakes.

Western blueberry *(V. uliginosum)*: This blue-black berry with a slate-gray bloom grows in bogs and in the coastal mountains.

Cultivated blueberries: More than 50 varieties of blueberries are cultivated in the Northwest. The first varieties available are Earliblue and Bluetta. Spartan, Bluecrop, Berkeley, and Elliot are available mid- to late season.

ZABAGLIONE
with Figs, Blackberries, and Honey Sauce

Pazzo Ristorante, Portland, Oregon

Few desserts are as ethereal yet satisfying as a traditional Italian
zabaglione—a rich egg custard flavored with marsala wine. Pastry chef Lee Posey
takes zabaglione several steps closer to heaven with the addition of fresh figs, blackberries, and a citrus-enhanced honey sauce. When fresh figs aren't available,
use large strawberries or other seasonal fruits.

6 large or 12 small fresh figs | *6 edible flowers, such as nasturtiums or violets*
1 pint fresh blackberries or marionberries |

ZABAGLIONE

4 egg yolks | *¼ cup marsala*
¼ cup sugar | *½ cup whipping cream*

HONEY SAUCE

1 cup white wine | *2 tablespoons freshly squeezed lemon juice*
½ cup honey | *½ vanilla bean, or 1 teaspoon vanilla extract*
¼ cup freshly squeezed orange juice |

CHILL 6 dessert plates.

FOR THE ZABAGLIONE, whisk together the egg yolks, sugar, and marsala in a large,
heatproof bowl. Set the bowl over a pan of simmering (not boiling) water, and whisk
the mixture constantly until it has about tripled in volume, 8 to 10 minutes. Remove
the bowl from the pan and set it in a shallow pan of ice water. Continue whisking until
the mixture is cool. Whip the cream until soft peaks form, then fold the cream into the
egg mixture. Refrigerate until needed, up to 6 hours before serving.

FOR THE HONEY SAUCE, combine the white wine, honey, orange juice, and lemon juice in a small saucepan with the vanilla extract, if using. If using a vanilla bean, slit the half bean lengthwise, scrape out the seeds, and add them to the pan with the split bean. Bring the mixture to a boil over medium heat, and boil until the sauce is reduced to the consistency of maple syrup, about 20 minutes (it will continue to thicken as it cools). Remove and discard the split vanilla bean and pour the sauce into a bowl. Cover and refrigerate until needed.

JUST BEFORE SERVING, cut large figs into 4 wedges, small figs in half. Spoon the chilled zabaglione onto the center of the chilled plates. Arrange the figs and berries around the zabaglione and drizzle the honey sauce over all. Garnish each plate with an edible flower and serve immediately.

Makes 6 servings

WHITE CHOCOLATE MOUSSE

with Crisp Cocoa Meringues and Raspberry Lemon Coulis

Beach Side Cafe, West Vancouver, British Columbia

Here is an ethereal combination of silky white chocolate mousse served with crisp, airy cocoa meringues. Look for the best-quality white chocolate you can find, such as Callebaut or Nestlé. It really makes a difference.

3 egg whites	*2 tablespoons unsweetened cocoa powder*
½ cup powdered sugar, plus more for garnish	*Mint sprigs, for garnish*

WHITE CHOCOLATE MOUSSE

5 ounces white chocolate, preferably Belgian, coarsely chopped	*1 cup whipping cream*

RASPBERRY LEMON COULIS

½ pound raspberries (fresh or frozen unsweetened)	*Juice and grated zest of 1 lemon*
	¼ cup powdered sugar

PREHEAT THE OVEN to 200°F. Line a baking sheet with parchment paper and trace eight 3-inch circles on the paper.

WHIP THE EGG WHITES in a mixer with ¼ cup of the sugar until soft peaks form. Add the remaining ¼ cup sugar and continue beating just until the meringue is stiff and glossy. Add the cocoa powder and mix until thoroughly combined.

SPOON THE MERINGUE into a pastry bag fitted with a large star or plain tip. Pipe the meringue into circles on the prepared sheet, starting in the center and working outward in a spiral. Bake the meringues until very dry, about 2 hours. When done, the meringues should lift easily from the paper. Let dry on a wire rack, then store in an airtight container until needed.

FOR THE WHITE CHOCOLATE MOUSSE, combine the chocolate with 2 table-spoons of the cream in the top of a double boiler or in a stainless steel bowl. Set the chocolate over a pan of gently simmering water and heat, stirring occasionally, until melted. Remove from the hot water and let cool slightly.

WHIP THE REMAINING cream until soft peaks form. Stir half of the whipped cream into the melted chocolate. Gently fold in the remaining whipped cream. Chill until needed, preferably at least 2 hours.

FOR THE COULIS, combine the raspberries, lemon juice, lemon zest, and sugar in a small pan and cook over low heat until the berries begin to fall apart. Transfer the mixture to a food processor or blender and purée. Pass the coulis through a strainer to remove the seeds, and refrigerate until needed.

TO ASSEMBLE THE DESSERT, set 1 meringue on each of 4 individual plates. Pipe or spoon some of the white chocolate mousse onto each round and set another meringue on top, gently pressing it down. Sprinkle the tops with powdered sugar and garnish each with a sprig of mint. Drizzle the coulis around the meringues and serve.

Makes 4 servings

WILD BLACKBERRY SORBET

Eagles Nest Inn, Langley, Washington

Native wild trailing blackberries are the favorite berry at the
Eagles Nest Inn Bed and Breakfast. Unsweetened frozen blackberries can
be used in place of fresh berries, but avoid berries frozen in syrup.

2 pints (4 cups) wild blackberries
1½ cups water
½ cup freshly squeezed orange juice
½ cup sugar

2 egg whites
Whole blackberries and thoroughly washed
blackberry leaves, for garnish (optional)

RINSE THE BERRIES and put them in a medium saucepan with the water, orange
juice, and sugar. Bring to a boil and simmer for 5 minutes. Strain off and reserve the
liquid. Press the fruit through a fine sieve, using a rubber spatula or the back of a large
spoon. Add this fruit purée to the reserved liquid and let cool to room temperature.

WHEN THE BLACKBERRY MIXTURE is cool, beat the egg whites until just stiff
but not dry. While gently beating, slowly pour in the blackberry mixture until fully incorporated. Pour the sorbet base into an ice cream maker and freeze according to the
manufacturer's instructions. When set, transfer the mixture to a freezer container and
continue freezing until solid. Before serving, let the sorbet sit at room temperature for
a few minutes to make scooping easier.

Makes 2 quarts

Unlike many fruits that ripen on the tree, pears must be picked unripe and allowed to ripen gradually at room temperature. The best way to ripen a pear is in a paper bag along with bananas or apples, which release ethylene gas that speeds the ripening process.

A pear's peak window of ripening passes very quickly—some chefs estimate it to be a mere two hours—so it's crucial to check pears often for ripeness by smelling them (ripe pears give off a delicious perfume) and by pressing down gently on the stem end. When ripe, a pear will give slightly.

Ninety-five percent of all pears grown in the United States come from Oregon, Washington, and Northern California. Others are grown in British Columbia's Okanagan Valley. Each variety has its own unique flavor and texture.

Bartlett: This is the pear most commonly grown in the Northwest. Fresh Bartletts, with their sweet, delicate flavor, are at their peak in summer, when their deep yellow skin is often flecked with pink or green.

Red Bartlett: A Yakima farmer was walking down a row of green Bartlett pears when he noticed a branch bearing red pears. Graftings taken from this tree (and a similar tree in Australia) are the ancestors of all red Bartletts. The flavor of these late-summer fruits is very similar to that of yellow Bartletts—delicate and sweet.

Bosc: Slow to ripen, this pear is often mistakenly thought of as tough and dry. But when ripe it is creamy, juicy, aromatic, and spicy. Often called the Fall's Russet by pear shippers, the Bosc is a favorite for eating fresh or for poaching, which shows off its elegant, graceful shape.

Comice: Many consider plump, fat-bottomed Comice pears to be the most delicious of all. They are raised to perfection in Oregon's Rogue River Valley.

Winter Nelis: According to one pear aficionado, this pear is "rough outside, but with a heart of gold." Its creamy, sweet, aromatic flesh is great for fresh eating and for baking in pies and tarts.

Seckel: Because of their small size and homey appearance, Seckels are not often sold commercially, but they are some of the tastiest pears around. Their dense flesh is particularly sweet, making them ideal as dessert pears or snacks.

PEAR-ALMOND TART

The Pewter Pot, Cashmere, Washington

The Pewter Pot restaurant sits in the heart of one of the world's premier pear-growing regions, Washington's Wenatchee Valley. Owner Kristi Biornstad features local d'Anjou or Bosc pears in this classic recipe. She suggests serving this tart at room temperature with whipped cream or vanilla ice cream. A glass of late harvest Northwest riesling or gewürztraminer wouldn't be a bad addition either.

1½ cups blanched almonds	*¼ teaspoon salt*
2 tablespoons all-purpose flour	*¼ teaspoon almond extract*
3 eggs	*1 large or 2 small ripe d'Anjou or Bosc pears*
½ cup packed brown sugar	*Whipped cream*
½ cup light corn syrup	

PASTRY DOUGH

6 tablespoons butter	*Pinch salt*
1½ cups all-purpose flour	*5 to 6 tablespoons chilled water*

FOR THE PASTRY DOUGH, cut the butter into the flour until it has the texture of coarse crumbs. Stir in the salt, followed by just enough water to form a supple dough. Lightly work the dough with the palm of your hand for about 30 seconds to ensure that it is well mixed. Wrap the dough and chill it for 30 minutes, then roll it into a 14-inch circle. Fold the dough into quarters and set it in an 11-inch tart tin with a removable bottom. Unfold and gently ease the dough to the edges of the tin with your fingertips; use a small knife to cut off any excess dough at the rim. Freeze the pastry shell until needed.

PREHEAT THE OVEN to 375°F.

COMBINE THE ALMONDS and flour in a food processor and process until finely chopped. Transfer to a bowl and set aside. Put the eggs, brown sugar, corn syrup, salt, and almond extract in the food processor and pulse just until smooth. Add the almond mixture and pulse until just blended, about 8 short pulses. Pour the mixture into the prepared pastry shell.

CORE THE PEAR, peel it, and cut it into about 20 thin slices. Arrange the pear slices in a circle over the filling, with the broader edges of the slices toward the outside of the tart. Bake the tart until the filling is set, 45 to 50 minutes. If the edges of the tart begin to brown before the center is cooked, cover it loosely with foil. Let the tart cool completely before serving. Remove the outer rim of the tart tin, cut the tart into wedges, and serve with a dollop of whipped cream.

Makes 8 to 12 servings

HOOD RIVER PEARS
Poached in Riesling and Wrapped in Phyllo

Columbia Gorge Hotel, Hood River, Oregon

Chefs at the Columbia Gorge Hotel use an ultra-sweet Northwest late
harvest riesling for poaching. They also suggest Portland-based Clear Creek
Distillery's pear brandy for use in the poaching liquid and the sauce. Virtually any
pears work well in this recipe, including Bartlett, Bosc, Comice, d'Anjou, and Seckel.
Tip: Once sheets of phyllo dough are removed from the package, keep them
covered with plastic wrap or a damp cloth to keep them moist and pliable.

6 cups (2 bottles) riesling	*1 vanilla bean, split, or*
1 cup sugar	*2 teaspoons vanilla extract*
Zest of 1 lemon, in 1-inch strips	*¼ teaspoon ground nutmeg*
3 tablespoons pear brandy	*4 small pears, peeled and cored whole*
1 small cinnamon stick	*4 sheets phyllo dough*
4 whole cloves	*¼ cup butter, melted*

SAUCE

¾ cup whipping cream	*3 tablespoons pear brandy*
2 egg yolks	*¼ cup sugar*

COMBINE THE WINE, sugar, lemon zest, pear brandy, cinnamon stick, cloves, vanilla
bean or extract, and nutmeg in a deep saucepan. Bring just to a boil, stirring occasionally,
then reduce to a simmer. Add the pears and cook gently over medium heat until they are
just tender when pierced with a knife, 40 to 45 minutes. Remove the pears from the
saucepan and drain. Strain the poaching liquid, return it to the saucepan, and boil until
reduced to about ¼ cup, about 30 minutes. Remove from the heat and let cool.

FOR THE SAUCE, whip the cream until soft peaks form; set aside. In the top of a double boiler or in a stainless steel mixing bowl, combine the egg yolks, brandy, reduced poaching liquid, and sugar. Whisk the mixture over a pan of lightly simmering water until it is thick and slightly warm, 3 to 5 minutes. Do not let the mixture become too hot or the eggs will curdle. When thick, remove the mixture from the heat and continue whisking until very light, 3 to 5 minutes longer. Whisk in about one-third of the whipped cream, then gently fold in the remaining whipped cream. Chill the sauce until needed.

PREHEAT THE OVEN to 400°F.

LAY 1 SHEET of phyllo dough on the work surface and gently brush some of the melted butter on it. Lay another sheet of phyllo on top and brush more butter on it. Repeat with the remaining phyllo sheets and butter. Cut the layered sheets into 4 equal portions and set a pear upright in the center of each portion. Lift the edges of the phyllo and gently press them against the pears; brush the outside of the phyllo with butter. Set the pears on a baking sheet and bake until the phyllo is nicely browned, about 8 minutes.

SET 1 PEAR in the center of each of 4 individual plates, and spoon the sauce around the pears. Serve immediately.

Makes 4 servings

PURE ESSENCE OF FRUIT

When you sniff a glass of Clear Creek Distillery's pear brandy, the essence of perfectly ripe Hood River Bartlett pears, rich and spicy, envelops your senses. "What you get in a bottle of brandy is pure condensed essence of fruit," says owner/distiller Stephen McCarthy. "We capture the wonderful qualities of the fruit in each bottle." This is easy to picture, when you consider that it takes more than 50 pears to produce a single bottle of pear brandy.

Listed as one of the top three distillers in the United States by wine and spirits writer Gerald Boyd, Stephen McCarthy first became enchanted with French pear brandy while traveling in Europe. When he learned that the Bartlett pears grown on his family's Hood River orchards were the same as those used to produce the famous Williams pear brandy of France, McCarthy decided to make his own Northwest version.

McCarthy studied distilling in Alsace, Switzerland, and Germany. Eventually he purchased an Alsatian still, specially designed to distill whole fruit into clear, unsweetened spirits or *eau de vie* ("water of life"). Located in Portland, Oregon, this is one of the few copper-pot distilleries operating in the United States.

Besides receiving kudos for his exceptional Clear Creek Distillery pear brandy, McCarthy has also gained international recognition for the exceptional quality of his apple brandy (produced from Golden Delicious apples and aged in Limousin Cognac barrels), grappas (made from the lees of grapes from the Adelsheim, Ponzi, and Eyrie Vineyards), kirsch (cherry brandy), framboise (raspberry liqueur), and others.

LUNA ICE CREAM

Cafe Luna, Shelton, Washington

This well may be the world's easiest homemade ice cream—nothing to cook, strain, or chill. Cafe Luna's former chef and owner, Victoria Benenate, said this recipe came from Nantucket, by way of her great-grandfather. Rich and delicious, this refreshing eggless ice cream is great on its own, but a warm chocolate sauce never hurt.

2 ripe bananas	Juice of 2 lemons (about ½ cup)
2 cups sugar	2 cups whipping cream
Juice of 2 oranges (about 1 cup)	2 cups milk

PURÉE THE BANANAS with the sugar in a blender or food processor until smooth. Transfer the mixture to a large bowl and stir in the orange juice, lemon juice, cream, and milk; blend until the sugar has dissolved.

POUR THE MIXTURE into an ice cream maker and freeze according to the manufacturer's instructions. Transfer to an airtight container and freeze until set, at least 2 hours.

Makes 2 quarts

APPLE BREAD PUDDING
with Brandy Butterscotch Sauce

Innisfree Restaurant, Glacier, Washington

Fred and Lynn Berman are organic farmers who opened a restaurant to showcase their favorite seasonal foods. Harvest time is Lynn Berman's favorite time of year, when she often turns crisp, tart apples into this homey bread pudding.

½ loaf sliced day-old bread (about 1 pound)	*1¼ cups packed dark brown sugar*
1½ to 2 pounds large apples	*2½ teaspoons ground cinnamon*
(preferably Jonagold, Spartan, or Melrose),	*1 teaspoon ground nutmeg*
cored and cut in ½-inch slices	*½ teaspoon ground cloves*
8 eggs	*1 cup ground hazelnuts*
5 cups half-and-half	

BRANDY BUTTERSCOTCH SAUCE

½ cup butter	*½ cup whipping cream*
½ cup honey	*¼ cup brandy*

PREHEAT THE OVEN to 350°F. Lightly grease a 9- by 13-inch baking dish.

CRUMBLE THE BREAD into coarse crumbs, using your hands. Sprinkle two-thirds of the crumbs into the prepared baking dish. Arrange the apple wedges over the bread in rows, overlapping them slightly.

COMBINE THE EGGS, half-and-half, 1 cup of the sugar, 2 teaspoons of the cinnamon, and the nutmeg and cloves in a large bowl. Beat well, then pour the mixture over the apples and bread. In another bowl, combine the ground hazelnuts with the remaining bread crumbs, ¼ cup brown sugar, and ½ teaspoon cinnamon. Sprinkle this mixture over the apples and press down gently so it soaks up some of the liquid. Bake until the pudding is lightly browned and a knife inserted in the center comes out clean, 60 to 70 minutes.

MAKE THE SAUCE while the bread pudding is baking. Combine the butter and honey in a deep, medium-sized saucepan (the mixture will expand when it boils) and heat over medium-low heat until both are melted and smooth. Bring to a boil without stirring and simmer for 5 minutes. Reduce the heat and carefully stir in the cream and brandy. Cook 1 minute longer. Set aside and keep warm until needed.

LET THE BREAD PUDDING sit for a few minutes before cutting into serving pieces. Drizzle a little of the brandy butterscotch sauce over each serving, passing the extra sauce separately.

Makes 12 servings

BAY LEAF CRÈME BRÛLÉE

The Herbfarm, Fall City, Washington

Chef Jerry Traunfeld loves the nutmeglike flavor that fresh bay leaves impart to dishes. Like many herbs, he explains, bay leaves have a notably different quality when used fresh rather than dried. Look for fragrant bay laurel trees at your favorite nursery if you'd like to grow your own. Other herbs lend themselves to this recipe as well, including lavender, rosemary, and rose geranium.

Traunfeld suggests using superfine sugar for caramelizing the tops of these custards because the fine grains melt and caramelize more evenly. You can buy it, or pulverize granulated sugar in your food processor or blender.

2 cups milk	3 whole eggs
2 cups whipping cream	5 egg yolks
12 fresh bay leaves	¾ cup granulated sugar
½ vanilla bean, split, or 1 teaspoon	Pinch salt
vanilla extract	½ cup superfine sugar

BRING THE MILK and cream to a boil in a medium saucepan over medium heat. Coarsely tear the fresh bay leaves and add them to the mixture along with the vanilla bean, if using. Remove the pan from the heat and let steep for 1 hour.

PREHEAT THE OVEN to 325°F.

BEAT THE EGGS, egg yolks, granulated sugar, vanilla extract (if using), and salt in a large bowl. Whisk in the steeped milk mixture until well blended. Strain the mixture through a fine sieve, discarding the bay leaves and vanilla bean.

POUR THE CUSTARD into eight ¾-cup ramekins and set them in a shallow pan filled with 1 inch of hot water. Bake the custards until just set but still slightly jiggly, 40 to 45 minutes. Let cool, then chill the custards for several hours or overnight.

JUST BEFORE SERVING, sprinkle the surface of each custard with superfine sugar, pouring off any excess. Using a small propane torch or your broiler, caramelize the sugar just until nicely browned. Serve immediately.

Makes 8 servings

NIGHTHAWK APPLEJACK CAKE

The Breadline Cafe, Omak, Washington

From the heart of cowboy country comes this flavorful apple and nut cake, spiked with a generous splash of Yukon Jack whiskey. "My grandfather was famous for his delightfully intoxicating applejack," recalls owner Paula Chambers of the Breadline Cafe. "My grandmother was always forced to secure a hidden cache of Grandpa Ed's precious liquor for use in this cake."

½ cup butter, melted
⅓ cup packed brown sugar
3 medium-sized tart apples
1 cup granulated sugar
½ cup chopped nuts
(such as walnuts, pecans, or hazelnuts)
1 egg, lightly beaten

2 tablespoons Yukon Jack whiskey,
*   plus more for serving*
2 teaspoons vanilla extract
1 cup all-purpose flour
1 teaspoon baking soda
½ teaspoon salt

PREHEAT THE OVEN to 350°F. Grease an 8- or 9-inch round cake pan.

COMBINE ¼ CUP of the melted butter with the brown sugar, stir to mix well, and pour into the cake pan. Peel, core, and thinly slice one of the apples. Arrange the apple slices in the bottom of the pan and set aside.

PEEL, CORE, and coarsely chop the remaining 2 apples and put them in a large bowl with the remaining ¼ cup melted butter, the granulated sugar, nuts, egg, Yukon Jack, and vanilla. Stir to mix.

COMBINE THE FLOUR, baking soda, and salt in another bowl. Stir the dry ingredients into the apple mixture until well combined. Pour the batter into the cake pan and bake until a toothpick inserted in the center of the cake comes out clean, about 50 minutes. Allow the cake to rest for 10 minutes, then carefully turn it out onto a serving plate. Lace the top with a generous splash of Yukon Jack and serve.

Makes 6 to 8 servings

ESPRESSO CHEESECAKE

Turtleback Farm Inn, Orcas Island, Washington

A slice of indulgence is often good for the soul. Packed with everything we usually try to avoid—cream cheese, Kahlua, espresso, butter, and more—this luscious dessert is one that's tough to turn down.

8 ounces Oreo or other chocolate wafer cookies, finely crushed (about 2 cups)
¼ cup butter, melted
2 pounds cream cheese, softened
3 eggs
¾ cup packed brown sugar

½ cup sour cream
¼ cup Kahlua or other coffee liqueur
¼ cup strong espresso, cooled
1 teaspoon vanilla extract
¾ teaspoon salt

PREHEAT THE OVEN to 350°F. Lightly grease an 8- or 9-inch springform pan.

STIR TOGETHER the crushed cookies and melted butter. Press the crumb mixture evenly onto the bottom and sides of the springform pan. Set aside.

BEAT THE CREAM CHEESE in the large bowl of an electric mixer until smooth and creamy. Add the eggs, followed by the brown sugar, sour cream, Kahlua, espresso, vanilla, and salt. When thoroughly blended and smooth, pour the filling into the prepared crust and bake until set (the center should not shudder when the pan is gently shaken), 60 to 70 minutes. Let cool thoroughly, then chill overnight before serving. Remove the rim of the springform pan and cut the cheesecake into wedges to serve.

Makes 10 to 12 servings

PEANUT BUTTER PIE

Colophon Cafe, Bellingham, Washington

Enjoy this creamy peanut butter pie with a favorite book and you'll be true
to its origin—a popular bookstore cafe. Use a metal soup spoon to help press the
cookie crust into the pan (it won't stick to the crumbs as your fingers will).

1½ cups whipping cream | *½ teaspoon vanilla extract*
8 ounces cream cheese, softened | *¼ cup powdered sugar*
¾ cup chunky peanut butter | *4 ounces semisweet chocolate, coarsely chopped*
¾ cup packed brown sugar | *1 tablespoon chopped peanuts*

CHOCOLATE COOKIE CRUST

8 ounces Oreo or other chocolate wafer | *¼ cup butter, melted*
cookies, finely crushed (about 2 cups) |

PREHEAT THE OVEN to 350°F.

FOR THE COOKIE CRUST, combine the cookie crumbs and melted butter in a
bowl and mix well. Pour the mixture into an 8-inch pie pan and press it evenly onto
the bottom and sides. Bake until set, 7 to 10 minutes. Set aside to cool.

PUT 1 CUP of the whipping cream in a medium bowl, preferably stainless steel, and
freeze for 10 minutes. Meanwhile, beat the cream cheese, peanut butter, and brown sugar
together in another bowl until creamy.

TAKE THE WHIPPING CREAM from the freezer, add the vanilla, and beat on low speed for 2 minutes. Add the powdered sugar and beat on high speed until soft peaks form. Do not overbeat.

FOLD THE WHIPPED CREAM into the peanut butter mixture. Pour the filling into the crust, spreading the top evenly. Freeze for at least 3 hours.

WHEN THE PIE IS FROZEN, combine the chocolate and the remaining ½ cup whipping cream in a small microwave-safe bowl and microwave for 30 to 45 seconds. Stir until smooth; let cool. Or gently heat the chocolate and cream together in a small pan over medium-low heat until the chocolate is nearly melted; remove from the heat, stir until smooth, and let cool slightly.

TAKE THE FROZEN PIE from the freezer and spread the chocolate topping over it. Sprinkle the chopped peanuts on top before the chocolate sets. If not serving right away, return the pie to the freezer. One hour before serving, take the pie out of the freezer and put it in the refrigerator. Use a knife dipped in hot water to cut the pie; it is easier to cut if still partially frozen.

Makes 8 servings

PESCHE RIPIENE
(Italian Stuffed Peaches)

Villa Isola, Langley, Washington

Here's a dessert served for breakfast at Gwen and Gary Galeotti's Whidbey Island retreat, whenever local peaches are ripe. Slightly firm peaches work best for this recipe (they hold up better in baking). Amaretti cookies and coconut macaroons are available at specialty food stores.

6 medium peaches, halved and pitted, skin on
½ cup crushed plain coconut macaroons (about 4 macaroons)
½ cup crushed amaretti cookies (about 12 cookies)

1 egg, lightly beaten
½ cup marsala wine or amaretto liqueur
1 cup whipping cream
2 tablespoons butter, melted

PREHEAT THE OVEN to 325°F. Lightly grease a baking dish in which the peach halves will fit snugly.

SCOOP SOME of the flesh from each peach half, leaving about a ¼-inch shell. Put the flesh in a large bowl and mash it. Stir in the crushed cookies and egg, followed by the marsala.

SET THE PEACH halves in the baking dish and spoon the peach and cookie mixture into the shells. Bake the stuffed peaches until the filling is firm, 45 to 50 minutes.

WHILE THE PEACHES are baking, whip the cream to soft peaks. Chill until needed.

TAKE THE STUFFED PEACHES from the oven, drizzle the tops with the melted butter, and let sit for a few minutes before serving. Arrange 2 peach halves on each individual plate, add a generous dollop of whipped cream, and serve.

Makes 6 servings

Taste is just one of the wonderful peach sensations. There are the downy touch of the fuzzy skin on your lips, the soft texture of the flesh, the sweet juices that run down your chin, and the plump roundness of the fruit in your hand.

In the Northwest, peaches are raised extensively in the Yakima Valley and other regions east of the Cascades. They are also grown in Oregon's Willamette Valley, on Sauvie Island near Portland, and in the Okanagan Valley of British Columbia.

Peaches are either white- or yellow-fleshed and either cling or freestone. Cling peaches, in which the flesh clings to the pit, are used mostly for processing. Semifreestone and freestone peaches have pits that are easier to remove and are most often favored for fresh eating and baking. Nectarines, for those who don't like fuzz, are simply a variety of non- fuzzy peach.

Peaches sold in supermarkets are often picked way too early and stored until they become mealy. Peaches ripen best on the tree. When perfectly ripe, they drop from the tree at the merest touch of your hand—all warm, juicy, and ready to eat.

Look for plump, round peaches with bright color and no greenish tinge. Peaches should smell fragrant, and feel heavy and full in your hand. Avoid bruised or blemished fruit.

To make removing the skin easier, dip peaches in boiling water for about 20 seconds. Drop into cold water and peel.

RHUBARB CRUMBLE
with Buttermilk Ice Cream

Christina's, Orcas Island, Washington

The tang of buttermilk counterpoints the sweetness of this rhubarb crumble.
If you like the tart flavor of rhubarb, use the lesser amount of sugar suggested;
if you prefer it sweeter, use more.

2 pounds rhubarb, trimmed and cut into 1-inch pieces (about 8 cups)	1 cup rolled oats
2½ to 3 cups granulated sugar	½ cup butter, softened
½ cup ginger ale	½ cup all-purpose flour
½ cup cornstarch	1 teaspoon ground cinnamon
1 tablespoon grated or minced ginger	1 teaspoon ground cardamom
1 cup packed brown sugar	½ teaspoon ground cloves

BUTTERMILK ICE CREAM

2 cups whipping cream	2 cups sugar
6 egg yolks	1 vanilla bean, or 2 teaspoons vanilla extract
2 cups buttermilk	

FOR THE ICE CREAM, combine 1 cup of the whipping cream and the egg yolks in the top of a double boiler and set it over a pan of lightly simmering (not boiling) water. Gently heat the mixture, stirring constantly, until thickened and creamy. Remove from the heat. In another bowl, combine the remaining 1 cup whipping cream with the buttermilk and sugar. Split the vanilla bean and scrape its seeds into the bowl, discarding the rest of the vanilla bean, or add the vanilla extract. Stir in the hot mixture. Pour the mixture into an ice cream maker and freeze according to the manufacturer's instructions. Transfer to an airtight container and freeze until set.

PREHEAT THE OVEN to 350°F. Lightly grease a 9- by 13-inch baking dish.

TOSS TOGETHER THE RHUBARB, sugar (to taste), ginger ale, cornstarch, and ginger in a large bowl until the ingredients are well mixed and the cornstarch has dissolved. Spread evenly in the baking dish.

COMBINE THE BROWN SUGAR, oats, butter, flour, cinnamon, cardamom, and cloves in another bowl. Stir until thoroughly combined. Scatter the topping evenly over the rhubarb. Bake the crumble until the top is golden and the filling is bubbling around the edges, 60 to 70 minutes. Let cool slightly before cutting into serving pieces. Serve with a generous scoop of buttermilk ice cream.

Makes 8 servings

MONTE BIANCO

Il Bacio, Redmond, Washington

Sweet, starchy, and comforting, chestnuts evoke winter and its holiday festivities. Their sweet aroma recalls images of hot roasted chestnuts, cozy fires, and silvery snowfalls. Compared to other nuts, chestnuts are surprisingly low in fat and protein. When purchasing fresh chestnuts (which are available during the holiday season), look for plump, heavy nuts with a shiny shell. This mounded dessert is meant to be reminiscent of the Monte Bianco Alps.

2 pounds fresh chestnuts, or 1 pound canned
2 cups milk (more if needed)
½ teaspoon vanilla extract

1 cup superfine or regular granulated sugar
1 cup whipping cream
3 tablespoons powdered sugar

IF USING FRESH CHESTNUTS, make a small slit in each chestnut shell with a small, sharp knife. Boil the chestnuts in water to cover for 30 minutes. Drain the chestnuts and remove the shells and inner skins.

PUT THE CHESTNUTS in a saucepan, add enough milk to cover, add the vanilla, and bring to a boil. Cover and simmer over low heat until the chestnuts have absorbed the milk, 10 to 15 minutes. (Canned chestnuts may not absorb all of the milk; if so, drain off excess milk after 15 minutes.) Purée the chestnuts in a food processor or food mill.

COMBINE THE CHESTNUT PURÉE with the sugar in a saucepan and cook over medium heat, stirring constantly, until the mixture begins to come away from the sides of the pan, about 15 minutes. Remove from the heat and let cool.

ARRANGE THE CHESTNUT PURÉE in a mound on a serving plate. Whip the cream with the powdered sugar until soft peaks form. Frost the mound with the whipped cream, using a pastry bag fitted with a star tip, if desired. Serve right away or chill until ready to serve.

Makes 4 to 6 servings

SWEET POTATO HAZELNUT POUNDCAKE

Wildwood, Portland, Oregon

Dense, sweet, and moist, this poundcake is delicious served with vanilla ice cream or caramel sauce. Note that the sweet potato needs to be baked a day ahead. If you like, dust the cake with powdered sugar just before serving.

1 large sweet potato (about 1 pound)
1¾ cups all-purpose flour
½ teaspoon baking powder
½ teaspoon salt
½ teaspoon ground nutmeg
½ teaspoon ground cinnamon
1½ cups sugar

¾ cup unsalted butter, softened
3 eggs
1 teaspoon vanilla extract
½ cup buttermilk
2 tablespoons water
½ cup hazelnuts, toasted and chopped

THE DAY BEFORE making the cake, preheat the oven to 350°F. Bake the sweet potato until tender, 50 to 60 minutes. When the potato is cool enough to handle, remove the skin and put the flesh in a small strainer set over a bowl. Let sit overnight in the refrigerator to allow excess liquid to drip off. Mash the flesh until smooth.

PREHEAT THE OVEN to 350°F.

BUTTER A 12-INCH bundt pan. Sift together the flour, baking powder, salt, nutmeg, and cinnamon. In the bowl of an electric mixer, cream the sugar and butter for about 3 minutes, then add the eggs, one at a time, blending well after each addition. Stir in the vanilla extract.

COMBINE THE BUTTERMILK and water in a small bowl. Add this to the butter/sugar mixture, little by little, alternating with the dry ingredients, folding gently to incorporate each addition. Fold in the hazelnuts and mashed sweet potato last. Pour the batter into the prepared pan, spreading it out evenly. Bake until a toothpick inserted in the center comes out clean, 50 to 60 minutes. Let the cake cool, then invert it onto a platter for serving.

Makes 10 to 12 servings

APPENDIX:
RESTAURANTS & INNS

ABIGAIL'S HOTEL
906 McClure Street
Victoria, BC V8V 3E7
Canada
(604) 338-5363

AMY'S MANOR
BED & BREAKFAST
PO Box 411
Pateros, WA 98846
(509) 923-2334

AVALON GRILL
4630 SW Macadam
Portland, OR 97201
(503) 227-4630

THE BAGELRY
1319 Railroad Avenue
Bellingham, WA 98225
(360) 676-5288

BAY CAFE
Lopez Town
Lopez Island, WA 98261
(360) 468-3700

BAY HOUSE
PO Box 847
5911 SW Highway 101
Lincoln City, OR 97367
(541) 996-3222

BEACH SIDE CAFE
1362 Marine Drive
West Vancouver, BC V7T 1B5
Canada
(604) 925-1945

THE BEACONSFIELD INN
998 Humboldt Street
Victoria, BC V8V 2Z8
Canada
(604) 384-4044

BREADLINE CAFE
102 S Ash Street
Omak, WA 98841
(509) 826-5836

BUGATTI'S RISTORANTE
18740 Willamette Drive
West Linn, OR 97068
(503) 636-9555

CAFE LANGLEY
PO Box 851
113 1st Street
Langley, WA 98260
(360) 221-3090

CAFE LUNA
221 W Railroad Street
Shelton, WA 98584
(360) 427-8709

CANYON WAY RESTAURANT
AND BOOKSTORE
1216 SW Canyon Way
Newport, OR 97365
(541) 265-8319

THE CAPTAIN'S PALACE
309 Belleville Street
Victoria, BC V8V 1X2
Canada
(604) 388-9191

CHARLES AT
SMUGGLERS COVE
8340 53rd Avenue W
Mukilteo, WA 98275
(206) 347-2700

CHATEAU WHISTLER
RESORT
4599 Chateau Blvd
Whistler, BC V0N 1B0
Canada
(800) 441-1414
(604) 938-8000

CHEF BERNARD'S
INN AND RESTAURANT
170 Spokane Street
Kimberley, BC V1A 2E4
Canada
(604) 427-4820

CHRISTINA'S
Rt 1, Box 59A
Eastsound, WA 98245
(360) 376-4904

CINCIN
1154 Robson Street
Vancouver, BC V6E 1B5
Canada
(604) 688-7338

COLOPHON CAFE
1208 11th Street
Bellingham, WA 98225
(360) 647-0092

COLUMBIA GORGE HOTEL
4000 Westcliff Drive
Hood River, OR 97031
(800) 345-1921
(541) 386-5566

COMMENCEMENT BAY
BED & BREAKFAST
3312 N Union Avenue
Tacoma, WA 98407
(206) 752-8175

DELILAH'S
1739 Comox Street
Vancouver, BC V6G 1H7
Canada
(604) 687-3424

DURLACHER HOF
PO Box 1125
7055 Nesters Rd
Whistler, BC V0N 1B0
Canada
(604) 932-1924

DYKSTRA HOUSE
RESTAURANT
114 Birch Avenue
Grandview, WA 98930
(509) 882-2082

EAGLES NEST INN
BED & BREAKFAST
3236 E Saratoga Road
Langley, WA 98260
(360) 221-5331

ETTA'S SEAFOOD
2020 Western Avenue
Seattle, WA 98121
(206) 443-6000

FAIRBURN FARM
COUNTRY MANOR
RR 7, 3310 Jackson Road
Duncan, BC V9L 4W4
Canada
(604) 746-4637

FLYING L RANCH
25 Flying L Lane
Glenwood, WA 98619
(509) 364-3488

FRIDAY HARBOR HOUSE
PO Box 1385
130 West Street
Friday Harbor, WA 98250
(360) 378-8455

FULLERS (SEATTLE SHER-
ATON HOTEL AND TOWERS)
1400 6th Avenue
Seattle, WA 98101
(206) 447-5544

GIOVANNI'S ON PEARL
402 N Pearl
Ellensburg, WA 98926
(509) 962-2260

GIRAFFE RESTAURANT
15053 Marine Drive
White Rock, BC V4B 1C5
Canada
(604) 538-6878

THE GOOD LIFE:
A BAKERY AND
RESTAURANT
2113 Otter Point Road
Sooke, BC V0S 1N0
Canada
(604)642-6821

GOURMET BY THE SEA
4378 S Island Highway
Oyster Bay, BC V9H 1E8
Canada
(604) 923-5234

GRATEFUL BREAD BAKERY
AND RESTAURANT
34805 Brooten Road
Pacific City, OR 97135
(503) 965-7337

GREEN GABLES INN
922 Bonsella
Walla Walla, WA 99362
(509) 525-5501

GROVELAND COTTAGE
4861 Sequim Dungeness Way
Dungeness, WA 98382
(360) 683-3565

THE HEATHMAN HOTEL
1001 SW Broadway
Portland, OR 97205
(800) 551-0011
(503) 241-4100

THE HERBFARM
32804 Issaquah–Fall City
Road
Fall City, WA 98024
(206) 784-2222

HOLIDAY FARM
54455 McKenzie River Drive
Blue River, OR 97413
(541) 822-3715

IL BACIO
16564 Cleveland Street
Redmond, WA 98052
(206) 869-8815

IL BISTRO
93-A Pike Street
Seattle, WA 98101
(206) 682-3049

IL PIATTO
2348 SE Ankeny
Portland, OR 97214
(503) 236-4997

THE INN AT LANGLEY
PO Box 835
Langley, WA 98260
(360) 221-3033

INN AT LUDLOW BAY
PO Box 65460
Port Ludlow, WA 98365
(360) 437-0411

INN AT SWIFTS BAY
Rt 2, #3402
Lopez Island, WA 98261
(360) 468-3636

INNISFREE RESTAURANT
9393 Mt. Baker Highway
Glacier, WA 98244
(360) 599-2373
(360) 599-2442

JAKE'S FAMOUS
CRAWFISH RESTAURANT
401 SW 12th Avenue
Portland, OR 97205
(503) 226-1419

JOT'S RESORT
PO Box J
Gold Beach, OR 97444
(800) 367-5687
(541) 247-6676

THE KALEENKA
1933 1st Avenue
Seattle, WA 98101
(206) 728-1278

KASPAR'S
19 W Harrison
Seattle, WA 98119
(206) 298-0123

KASTEEL FRANSSEN
(AULD HOLLAND INN)
5681 SR 20
Oak Harbor, WA 98277
(360) 675-2288

LA BERENGERIE
Montague Harbour Road
Galiano Island, BC V0N 1P0
Canada
(604) 539-5392

LA MARGARITA COMPANY
545 Ferry Street SE
Salem, OR 97301
(503) 362-8861

LA SERRE RESTAURANT
PO Box 286
160 W 2nd
Yachats, OR 97498
(541) 547-3420

MAPLE LEAF GRILL
8909 Roosevelt Way NE
Seattle, WA 98115
(206) 523-8449

MARCO'S SUPPERCLUB
2510 1st Avenue
Seattle, WA 98121
(206) 441-7801

MARQUEE HOUSE
333 Wyatt Court NE
Salem, OR 97301
(503) 391-0837

MCCORMICK'S FISH
HOUSE AND BAR
722 4th Avenue
Seattle, WA 98104
(206) 682-3900

MOUNT ASHLAND INN
550 Mt. Ashland Road
Ashland, OR 97520
(541) 482-8707

NEARLY NORMAL'S
109 NW 15th Street
Corvallis, OR 97330
(541) 753-0791

OCEANWOOD
COUNTRY INN
630 Dinner Bay Road
Mayne Island, BC V0N 2J0
Canada
(604) 539-5074

THE OLD FARMHOUSE
RR 4, 1077 North End Road
Salt Spring Island, BC
V0S 1E0
Canada
(604) 527-4113

OLYMPIC LIGHTS
4531-A Cattle Point Road
Friday Harbor, WA 98250
(360) 378-3186

PASSPORT
1509 Wall Street
Everett, WA 98201
(206) 259-5037

PAZZO RISTORANTE
627 SW Washington Street
Portland, OR 97205
(503) 228-1515

THE PEWTER POT
124 Cottage Avenue
Cashmere, WA 98815
(509) 782-2036

QUIMPER INN
1306 Franklin Street
Port Townsend, WA
98368
(360) 385-1060

RAKU KUSHIYAKI
4422 W 10th Avenue
Vancouver, BC V6R 2H9
Canada
(604) 222-8188

RAM'S HEAD INN
Box 636
Rossland, BC V0G 1Y0
Canada
(604) 362-9577

RAY'S BOATHOUSE
6049 Seaview Avenue NW
Seattle, WA 98107
(206) 789-3770

THE RIO CAFE
125 9th Street
Astoria, OR 97103
(503) 325-2409

RIVERPLACE HOTEL
1510 SW Harbor Way
Portland, OR 97201
(800) 227-1333
(503) 228-3233

RIVER RUN COTTAGES
  4551 River Road W
  Ladner, BC V4K 1R9
  Canada
  (604) 946-7778

ROBERTO'S RESTAURANT
  PO Box 2806
  205 A Street
  Friday Harbor, WA 98250-
  9590
  (360) 378-6333

ROMEO INN
  295 Idaho Street
  Ashland, OR 97520
  (541) 488-0884

ROVER'S
  2808 E Madison Street
  Seattle, WA 98112
  (206) 325-7442

SALISBURY HOUSE
  750 16th Avenue E
  Seattle, WA 98112
  (206) 328-8682

SALMON HOUSE
ON THE HILL
  2229 Folkestone Way
  West Vancouver, BC V7S 2Y6
  Canada
  (604) 926-3212

SOL DUC HOT SPRINGS
  PO Box 2169
  Port Angeles, WA 98362
  (360) 327-3583

STATE STREET INN
  1005 State Street
  Hood River, OR 97031
  (541) 386-1899

STEPHANIE INN
  PO Box 219
  Cannon Beach, OR 97110
  or
  2740 S Pacific
  Tolovana Park, OR 97145
  (800) 633-3466
  (503) 436-2221

STONEHEDGE INN
  3405 Cascade Drive
  Hood River, OR 97031
  (541) 386-3940

THE SUTTON
PLACE HOTEL
  845 Burrard Street
  Vancouver, BC V6Z 2K6
  Canada
  (604) 682-5511

SYLVIA BEACH HOTEL
  267 NW Cliff
  Newport, OR 97365
  (541) 265-5428

TOKELAND HOTEL AND
RESTAURANT
  100 Hotel Road
  Tokeland, WA 98590
  (360) 267-7006

TURTLEBACK FARM INN
  Rt 1, Box 650
  Eastsound, WA 98245
  (360) 376-4914

VILLA ISOLA
  5489 S Coles Rd
  Langley, WA 98260
  (360) 221-5052

WATERFRONT
CENTRE HOTEL
  900 Canada Place Way
  Vancouver, BC V6C 3L5
  Canada
  (800) 441-1414
  (604) 691-1991

WHARFSIDE
BED & BREAKFAST
  PO Box 1212
  Friday Harbor, WA 98250
  (360) 378-5661

THE WHITE SWAN
GUEST HOUSE
  1388 Moore Road
  Mt. Vernon, WA 98273
  (360) 445-6805

WILDWOOD
  1221 NW 21st Avenue
  Portland, OR 97209
  (503) 248-9663

INDEX

C

Caesar Salad, Northwest, 99
Cafe Langley, 80, 122–23, 235
Cafe Luna, 54–55, 190–91, 219, 235
Cake
  Nighthawk Applejack Cake, 224
  Sweet Potato Hazelnut Poundcake, 233. *See also* Baked treats
Calamari Neapolitan Style, 58
Canyon Way Restaurant and Bookstore, 115, 235
The Captain's Palace, 186, 235
Caretto d'Agnello, 140–41
Celery root, with mashed potatoes 162–63
Cereals
  Groveland Cottage Hot Cereal, 9
  "Nutty But Nice" Granola, 23
Chanterelle mushrooms, 16, 130, 131
  Chanterelle Risotto Cakes, 192–93
  Chanterelle Salad, 172–73. *See also* Mushrooms
Charles at Smuggler's Cove, 121, 235
Chateau Whistler Resort, 117, 235
Cheese
  Corn and Cheese Chowder, 93
  Frisée with Red Beets and Blue Cheese, 108
  goat cheese, 65, 102
  Grilled Crab and Cheddar Sandwich, 181
  Lemon Cheese Braid, 24–25
  Tomato Cheddar Dill Bread, 111
Cheesecake
  Espresso Cheesecake, 225
  Garlic Cheesecake, 72–73
Chef Bernard's Inn and Restaurant, 74, 144–45, 235
Chestnuts, Monte Bianco, 232
Chicken, 106, 126. *See also* Quail
  Basic Chicken Stock, 81
  Circassian, 122
  Forest Chicken, 130–31
  Hazelnut Chicken Breasts, 124–25
  Hearts of Romaine with Chicken, 109
  Herbal Tea-Smoked Chicken Breast, 128

in Paprika-Laced Walnut Sauce, 122–23
  Poulet aux Crevettes, 121
Chiles, 60, 64, 126, 166, 144, 176, 182, 184
  in Confetti Garden Salsa, 40
  Red Chile Garlic Salsa, 166–67
  hotness, varieties, 40
  Red Chile Garlic Salsa, 166–67
Chinese Greens, Wok-Seared, 146–47
Chives
  Chive Cornmeal Crackers, 50–51
  Chive Potato Pancakes, 4–5
Chocolate
  Chocolate Soufflé Tarts, 204–05
  Cookie Crust for Peanut Butter Pie, 226
  White Chocolate Mousse with Crisp Cocoa Meringues, 210–11
Chowders
  Corn and Cheese Chowder, 93
  Mussels in Corn Chowder, 88–89. *See also* Soups
Christina's, 106–07, 230–31, 235
Cilantro
  Red Onion Cilantro Relish, 152–53. *See also* Herbs
CinCin, 129, 136–37, 235
Cinnamon Buns, 14–15
Cioppino d'Oro, 178–79
Clams, 37, 177
  Malaysian Clams, 74
  Manila, 37, 74, 177
  razor, 69
  Sautéed Razor Clams, 68–69
  Steamed Clams Sol Duc, 37
  varieties, storage, 177. *See also* Shellfish dishes
Cocoa Meringues, Crisp, 210–11
Coffee. *See* Espresso
Colophon Cafe, 99, 226–27, 235
Colophon Croutons, 99
Columbia Gorge Hotel, 112, 172–73, 216–17, 236
Commencement Bay Bed & Breakfast, 22, 236
Confetti Garden Salsa, 40
Cookies, 225
  Chocolate Cookie Crust, 226
  Crisp Cocoa Meringues, 210–11
  Espresso Cookies, 200–01
Coriander, fresh. *See* Cilantro

Corn
  Chive Cornmeal Crackers, 50–51
  Corn and Cheese Chowder, 93
  in Four Seasons Baked Eggs, Summer, 20–21
  Polenta-Encrusted Crab, 70–71
Cottage cheese topping for pancakes, 4–5
Coulis
  Fresh Tomato Coulis, 162–63
  Raspberry Lemon Coulis, 210–11
Couscous, Shiitake Mushroom, 132–33
Crab
  and Avocado Hoppa Rolls, 64–65
  Polenta-Encrusted, 70–71. *See also* Dungeness crab, Shellfish dishes
Crab and Avocado Hoppa Rolls, 64–65
Crab Cakes, Dungeness, 184–85
Crackers, Chive Cornmeal, 50–51
Cranberries
  Cranberry Pot Roast, 148–49
  Cranberry-Apple Bette, 202–03
  history, nutrients, storage, 203
  Winter Fruit Compote, 19
Crawfish
  Linguine with Crawfish and Fire Sauce, 182–83
  Cream cheese filling, Lemon Cheese Braid, 24–35
  Lemon Cream Cheese-Stuffed French Toast, 32–33
  Warm Salmon Spread, 56–57. *See also* Cheesecake
Cream soups. *See* Soups
Creamy Onion Soup with Bay Shrimp, 92
Crepes
  for Crab and Avocado Hoppa Rolls, 64–65
  Gingerbread, with Apple Filling, 12
Crème brûlée
  Bay Leaf Crème Brûlée, 222–23
  Espresso Crème Brûlée, 200–01
  Garlic and Thyme Crème Brûlée, 50–51
Crisp Cocoa Meringues, 210–11
Croutons, Colophon, 99
Curry Yogurt Sauce, 144–45
Custards. *See* Crème Brûlée

ABOUT THE AUTHORS

Cynthia C. Nims is the food editor of *Simply Seafood* and *Spa* magazines. She holds the Grand Diplôme d'Etudes Culinaires from La Varenne cooking school in France, and served as editorial assistant to Patricia Wells in Paris.

Lori McKean, author of *Pacific Northwest Flavors*, is a former chef and cooking teacher who studied at the Ballymaloe Cookery School in Ireland. She has served as food editor for *Northwest Palate* magazine and is currently contributing editor to *Regions Northwest*. Her articles on food and wine have appeared in *Bon Appétit*, *Better Homes & Gardens*, and *The Wine Enthusiast*, among others.